REMEMBER ME TO ALL KI

The Bolton men who lost their lives in the Galli

"We leave tomorrow, June 10th., for the fighting again - my second time on earth. I cannot say very much, as I feel a bit upset about leaving tomorrow. Remember me to all kind friends who inquire after me."

Lance Corporal Frederick Ribchester 2474
1st Bn Lancashire Fusiliers
Killed in action, Gallipoli, 28 June 1915

Acknowledgements

'Remember Me To All Kind Friends' has been underwritten by the several Ex-Servicemen's and Women's organisations in Bolton through funds raised by the annual Bolton Remembrance Concert.

We are also very grateful to the following for their invauable support in the preparation of this publication:

Bolton at Home • Rumworth School • The Gallipoli Association

*This book has been produced by **DBBC** and is based on our Heritage Lottery funded project **Tracing Your Roots to Gallipoli** where our young students researched the lives of over 180 Bolton soldiers who died as a result of the Gallipoli campaign of 1915.*

Thanks to...

- **DBBC students** for their research work

- **The Heritage Lottery Fund** for supporting the original project
- **Bolton Library and Museum Service** for their advice and resources
- **The Fusilier Museum** at Bury for providing some of the names of soldiers killed at Gallipoli
- **Lancashire Infantry Museum**, Fulwood Barracks Preston for their support
- **Kim Phillips** - The Spirits of Gallipoli Project, Australia for extra information about AIF casualties
- **Many** individuals in Bolton and beyond for their interest and stories
- **The Bolton News** for their coverage
- **Anne Wilson** for her constant support and in-depth research with the students
- **Alan Markland** for his background knowledge of the subject and for inspiring the young people
- **The Bolton Journal and Guardian**, 29 December 1916 for providing us with the inspiration!

Design and additional research by **Brian Mills** • www.bmillsdesigns.co.uk

Printed by **The Print Room, Bolton** • www.theprintroom.me.uk

Introduction

Between April 1915 and January 1916 the Gallipoli campaign cost the lives of well over 56,000 Allied servicemen and a similar number of Turkish troops of the Ottoman Empire.

Many of the British recruits were drawn from the mills, collieries and factories of the north of England and Lancashire in particular.

At least 190 men from Bolton were among those who never returned home. They served mostly with the Loyal North Lancashire Regiment, the Lancashire Fusiliers and the Border Regiment, who all recruited extensively in the area, but many other units were also represented.

From little piecers to clerks, footballers to Sunday School teachers, they were all someone's son, brother, husband or father.

This book is an attempt to honour their memory by recording who they were and where they came from.

The inspiration for the original project came from the chance purchase of a fragile and yellowing supplement of the Bolton Journal and Guardian from December 1916 which gathered together 800 photographs of many of the local men who had been killed in the first two years of the First World War.

We thought it would make an interesting project for some of our young students to find out more about the people behind the pictures - many of whom were only a few years older than themselves at the time of their deaths.

We limited our researches to the Gallipoli campaign as it had a clearly defined beginning and end - and would (so we thought) be a manageable number.

We confined ourselves to the boundaries of the current Bolton Borough and used the same criteria that the original Bolton Roll of Honour used: individuals included should have been born in in the Borough or been resident at the time of enlistment or have some other significant connection with the Borough.

Local newspapers of the period carried short articles each week about war deaths which provided vital clues for further research and allowed us to identify individuals as they appeared on census returns and other records.

Where available, these newspaper stories have been reproduced verbatim - complete with archaic punctuation.

The stories usually originated via a relative of the deceased contacting the newspaper at the time, so if no contact was made then no article appeared which in turn made research more difficult. Without additional information some names were so locally common that it was impossible to choose the correct person from several similar candidates. As anyone who has ever dabbled in family history research will tell you, there are also some people who somehow managed to avoid appearing on the Census returns or elsewhere.

Many service records of British soldiers in the First World War were destroyed in an air raid during the Second World War but we have referred to them where they have survived.

The Commonwealth War Graves Commission (CWGC) website at www.cwgc.org was also an invaluable resource.

This has been a major undertaking for us. We will have made mistakes - hopefully not too many - and we are confident that we will have omitted names of individuals who ought to be here.

If you have any more information, additions or amendments to suggest we would be happy to consider them for the online version of the Roll of Honour which is at:

www.bolton-gallipoli.org.uk

DBBC June 2014

Gallipoli 1915

By early 1915, following heavy defeats over the British Expeditionary Forces by the German Army, the British military strength was much reduced. A new army was needed and the task of raising it was given to Lord Horatio Herbert Kitchener who, as Secretary of State for War, under his famous banner headline "Your Country Needs You", rapidly increased the size of the army from a depleted twenty divisions to seventy.

A total of 100,000 new recruits made up the first six of these divisions (K1), and among them was the 13th (Western) Division of which the 6th Battalion, The Loyal North Lancashire Regiment (LNL), was a component.

The rank and file of this unit were enlisted directly from mills and factories in and around Bolton. In the British Army an infantry division is usually made up of 3 battalions of between 300 and a thousand soldiers, and a battalion can be further divided up into platoons, companies etc.

The Gallipoli campaign lasted less than 9 months. The final withdrawal from Gallipoli over a period of two weeks was a model for such future events as Dunkirk, and is often remembered as its only saving grace.

The residents of Australia and New Zealand remember their brave soldiers with immense pride and many of them return to Gallipoli on 25 April each year to mark Anzac Day.

Gallipoli was a defeat for Britain, and so it has become lost in our celebrations for other victories; it is only the families of loved ones who were killed that remember so vividly.

Collecting the kits of the dead and wounded on W Beach

Harold Greenhalgh: One soldier's story

Harold Greenhalgh was born to Lawrence and Sarah Frances Greenhalgh, née Ashton, on 28 March 1895 at 199 Darwen Road, Turton. The family moved house several times in the following 20 years.

This kind of constant removal, or 'flitting' as it was known, was not uncommon in those days following the introduction of mass production when families literally 'chased the cotton' as new mills opened up.

Harold attended school in Walmsley before going to work as a dyer at Bridson's bleachworks on Chorley Street, Bolton.

The 6th Battalion, LNL, was commissioned on 8 August 1914 and Harold signed on sometime between then and October 1914 when he is shown as a batman to Lieutenant Grimshaw at Tidworth Barracks, Salisbury plain, where initial training began.

From Tidworth the battalion moved to Blackdown near Aldershot, and on 14 June 1915 the whole of the 13th division (as well as the 10th and 11th) got the train at Farnborough station to go to Avonmouth where they were supposed to board the SS Japanese Prince. They were re-routed to the SS Braemar Castle instead and eventually sailed on 17 June, bound for Malta.

Their next port of call was Alexandria in Egypt for more training and acclimatisation. This is where Harold was instructed in how to use a machine gun.

Mudros is the major port on the Greek island of Lemnos and lies some 50 kilometres (30 miles) from the landing beaches of Gallipoli. It is here that the divisions rested and trained whilst waiting for the call for invasion.

The invasion of the Gallipoli peninsula was an entirely sea-borne operation. It has to be remembered that during that time no purpose-built landing ships existed. The main transport for men, mules, horses, artillery and all supplies was by barges towed by launches steered by 16-year old Royal Navy midshipmen, and by a variety of whatever craft was available. The hastily converted collier, SS River Clyde, having famously run herself ashore on V Beach in a one-off landing feat, remained stuck for the rest of the campaign.

During the night of 6 July 1915 the 6th LNLs were put ashore by lighter at Seghir Dere in Gully Ravine, where they went into bivouac.

Landing on V Beach

General Hamilton's immediate battle plans were severely handicapped by the fact that he was greatly under strength. His original force, landed on 25 April, had suffered heavy casualties and, with some divisions not yet arrived, it is doubtful that he had more than a mere 110,000 men for the operation. This was to reinforce the Australians and New Zealanders at Anzac Cove, to effect a landing at Suvla Bay and from there to attempt the capture of the main peak of Sari Bair, thus overlooking and commanding the narrows of the Dardanelles. The 6th Battalion LNL was sent forward immediately into the front line, relieving troops of the 29th Division.

The 6th Battalion LNL returned to Anzac Cove on 4 August and occupied bivouac billets in Victoria Gully where, as a result of enemy shelling, two men were killed and a further 32 were injured.

On the night of 6 August two battalions of the 13th Division, of which the LNL was one, commenced their advance from Anzac Cove. On the following morning the 6th LNL was marched to the foot of the Chailuk Dere, and on the night of the next day it was sent to the Apex as reinforcement to the New Zealand Brigade.

On 9 August three columns were sent forward to complete the conquest of Chunuk Bair. During that night the worn out New Zealanders were relieved and the 6th Battalion LNL and the 5th Wiltshires took their places in inadequately shallow trenches.

The 6th Battalion LNL arrived first and set about trying to improve the poor shelter. The Turks realised that if the summit of Chunuk Bair was held, the outcome would be a massive Allied advantage. They therefore shelled the ridge at dawn on 9 and 10 August and then let loose a horde of infantry soldiers with fixed bayonets. Both the Wiltshires and the Lancashire boys had no chance - caught in the open they were swiftly and mercilessly overwhelmed by sheer weight of numbers. The battalions did all they could, Captain Mather's company (6th Battalion LNL) doing especially well charging 3 times with the bayonet.

The official despatch states: "The two battalions of the New Army chosen to hold Chunuk Bair were the 6th Loyal North Lancashire Regiment and the 5th Wiltshire Regiment. They were simply overwhelmed by a superior and determined foe."

General Sir Ian Hamilton later wrote: "Generals fought in the ranks, and men dropped their scientific weapons and caught one another by the throat. So desperate a fight cannot be described. The Turks came on again and again, fighting magnificently and calling on the name of Allah. Our men stood to it and maintained, by many a deed of daring, the old traditions of their race. There was no flinching. They died in the ranks where they stood."

It is interesting to note that the commander of the Turkish divisions in this battle was none other than Mustafa Kemal, later Kemal Atatürk, soon to be the father of a new Turkish nation. At a later stage in the battle of Chunuk Bair he is reputed to have halted the shooting saying, "We have killed enough. Shoot over their heads to keep them occupied." Unfortunately the continued firing set the gorse and bracken alight, resulting in many of the Lancashire and Wiltshire men being burned to death.

Some 450 men were lost at Chunuk Bair, most of whom have no known grave, but are remembered on the Helles Memorial.

Private **Harold Greenhalgh** from Bolton, Lancashire is one of them.

Memorial plaque for Harold Greenhalgh - commonly known as a Death Penny

Bolton men who lost their lives in the Gallipoli campaign by regiment / unit

Army Service Corps
Robert Hutchinson Booth

Army Veterinary Corps
Walter Alfred Singleton

Australian Imperial Force
Harry Alston
William Truman Altree
Jack Blackburn
Reuben Coop
Albert Robert Dawson
William Henry Lancaster
Harry Lomax

Border Regiment
Samuel Barlow
William Brittain
Charles Edward Casement
Percy Chapman
James Drury
Norman Edwardson
Robert Evans
Joseph Farnworth
Joseph Fisher
James Fox
Wright Glennerster
Albert Grundy
Thomas Marsden
George Alfred Naylor
Joseph Parker
James Ritchie
Matthew Reddy
William Robert Simpson
Albert Thornley
Albert Edward Varle
George Waddilove
James Walker
James Whitworth
John Wildman

Connaught Rangers
Reuben Caldwell
Thomas Westby

Duke of Lancaster's Own Yeomanry
John Dearden

East Lancashire Regiment
George Edwin Clark

Essex Regiment
Victor Collins Green
Thomas Hewitt
Henry Lowe

King's Own (Royal Lancaster Regt)
Walter Hilton
James Ratcliffe

King's Own Scottish Borderers
Walter Freeman

Lancashire Fusiliers
Thomas Baines
Thomas Belsey
James Bamford Bennett
John Birch
Thomas Blackledge
Richard Browitt
Alfred Carey
Alfred Carrington
Joseph Collier
Thomas Edge
John Fielding
Arthur Ellis Hardman
Thomas Ardill Haslam
Harry Hogg
Arthur Holden
Samuel Horrocks
Edward Houghton
John Jarvis
Thomas Kelly
John Leach
Joseph Lomax
Frank Lonsdale
Albert Lord
George Lyons
Henry Marsden
James Marsden
Martin McDermott
Joseph McKenna
John McLoughlin
George Edwin Melling
John Miller
Abraham Moscrop
William Morris
William Henry Nield
William Partington
Robert William Porter
John Preston
Frederick Ribchester
Edward Rimmer
James Scott
Peter Smith
Norman Thompson
Joseph Travers
Ernest Tunnah
Thomas Wilkinson
John Worsley
Tom Fletcher Yates

Loyal North Lancashire Regiment
William Barlow
Thomas Helme Byrne
William Shepherd Calderley
Joseph Calderley
Mark Coups
James Edmund Denton
James Dolan
James Doyle
Robert Durning
Harold Fairhurst
Albert Fisher
John Fisher
Matthew Fisher
Thomas Fishwick
James Flanagan
Thomas Flanagan
Roland Foster
William Glazebrook
Harold Greenhalgh
Arthur Hart
James Hatton
Ralph Horne
Andrew Howard
Frederick Howarth
Samuel Hulme
Andrew Jackson
William Lawrence
Roger Lindsay
Jonah Boyd Macdonald
John Robert Martland
James Mather
Hugh McCarthy
Alexander James McDowell
James Morris
Robert Norcross
Joseph Michael Philbin
John William Pitfield
Thomas Rothwell
William Sharples
Thomas Spencer
Richard Tickle
Robert Travis
Jesse Vickers
William Walker
William Henry Woodall
John William Worsley
Herbert Yates

Manchester Regiment
Joshua Bennett
Stanley Carter
John Gannon
James Hilton
Matthew Killoran
John Lowe
Samuel Pickvance
Harry Tatlow
Thomas Tither

Royal Army Medical Corps
John Edwin Carter
Samuel Gee
George Arthur Greenhalgh
Henry Newell
James Poole

Royal Dublin Fusiliers
James Grogan
William Henry Holden
John William Nightingale
John Joseph O'Brien
Thomas O'Brien
Cornelius Seeler
Robert Selkirk
George Taubman
Albert Edward Williams
Robert Wood

Royal Field Artillery
Henry Garner
Samuel Guffogg

Royal Irish Fusiliers
Edward Mullaney

Royal Inniskilling Fusiliers
William Nuttall

Royal Munster Fusiliers
Henry Parker

Royal Naval Division
Wilfred Almond
Arthur Beardsworth
Frederick Robert Bunce
Robert Derbyshire
Francis William Fisher
Albert Graham
William Hollas
John Scotson Jones
Richard Jones
James Norris
Joseph Smith
George Edward Stockham
William Wilson
Alan Woodley

South Lancashire Regiment
Thomas Stallard

South Wales Borderers
Stanley Gill
William Hodgkinson
George Warren

Welsh Regiment
Samuel Wolstencroft

Wilfred Almond

Bolton Journal and Guardian 20 August 1915

Young Astley Bridge Soldier Dies from Wounds

Mr. Lewis Almond, 2, Almond-st., Astley Bridge, has received news that his son, **Wilfred** died on Sunday, August 8th, in hospital at Alexandria from wounds received in the Dardanelles. Pte. Almond, who would have been 21 on Wednesday, enlisted in the R.M.L.I. Portsmouth Battalion, leaving England on February 27th for the Dardanelles. He was a scholar at St. Paul's, Astley Bridge, where he held the record for punctual and regular attendance, not being late or absent during the period from Nov. 23rd, 1900, to August 19th, 1908. Prior to enlisting he was an apprentice engineer for Messrs. Jno. Musgrave and Co., Ltd., and was a student at the technical classes, receiving a first class certificate for practical drawing. Much regret is felt in Astley Bridge, as news had been received recently that Pte. Almond was progressing nicely.

Wilfred was the son of Lewis Almond b.1861, a superintendent for the Refuge Insurance Co, and Jane Almond née Johnson b.1857.

The couple are listed on the 1891 Census living at 5 Rowland Street, Bolton with son John James b.1884 and daughter Bertha b.1887.

Wilfred appeared on the 1901 Census living with the family at 2 Almond Street, Bolton.

His mother died in 1909.

By the 1911 Census he was living with his father and sister at the Almond Street address.

Wilfred died in hospital from a gunshot wound to the head.

Name	Almond, Wilfred
Rank	Private
Number	PO/698(S)
Unit	Portsmouth Bn Royal Naval Division, Royal Marine Light Infantry
Born	Bolton, Lancashire August 1894
Enlisted	Manchester 19 October 1914
Died	Alexandria, Egypt 9 August 1915
Age	17
Grave or Memorial	Alexandria (Chatby) Military and War Cemetery, Egypt

Harry Alston

Barrier Miner (Broken Hill, NSW, Australia) 16 June 1915

PRIVATE HARRY ALSTON

News of the death, killed in action, of **Private Harry Alston**, of Broken Hill, has been received. Private Alston, who has a brother in Broken Hill, was working on the mines previous to the war. He was about 25 years of age. He resided as a boarder at the Royal Mail Hotel. He left with the first contingent.

Harry was the son of Thomas Alston b.1858, manager of a cotton spinning mill, and Harriett Alston née Cowley b.1854.

Harry first appeared on the 1891 Census living at 287 Park View, Bolton with his patents.

His mother, Harriett, died in September 1893.

His father remarried to Ellen Swain b.1871 at St Mark's Church, Bolton on 11 July 1894. Ellen was a school mistress by profession.

In 1901 he was living at 307 Lever Street, Bolton with his father, step-mother and brother Samuel b.1892 and half-sister Annie Gertrude b.1895.

By 1911 the family were living at 135 High Street, Bolton.

Harry was employed as a stripper and grinder in a cotton spinning mill.

Thomas Alston died in late 1911.

Harry served for three years as a Territorial with the Duke of Lancaster's Own Yeomanry.

At some point between 1911 and 1914 Harry and his brother Samuel emigrated to Australia.

Harry's medical examination on enlistment in the Army recorded him as being 5' 1/4" tall and weighing 150 lbs with a fresh complexion, brown eyes and auburn hair.

He embarked from Adelaide on 20 October 1914 on HMAT Ascanius.

He then spent 29 days in a military hospital in Cairo from 15 January 1914, being treated for pneumonia.

In his will he left his estate - including shares in Crosses and Winkworth Ltd (a Bolton cotton spinning company) - to his step-mother.

His personal belongings at the time of his death were listed as:

1 Note-Book

1 Testament

1 Belt

1 Cigarette-Case

1 Wristlet for Watch

1 Handkerchief

Name	Alston, Harry
Rank	Private
Number	591
Unit	10th Bn Australian Imperial Force
Born	Bolton, Lancashire 1889
Enlisted	Morphetville, South Australia 28 August 1914
Died	Gallipoli, Turkey 27 April 1915
Age	25
Grave or Memorial	Lone Pine Memorial, Gallipoli, Turkey

William Truman Altree

Bolton Journal and Guardian 1 October 1915

BOLTONIAN WITH THE AUSTRALIANS KILLED

Another youthful Boltonian, who was living in Australia at the outbreak of war, has lost his life in the severe fighting in Gallipoli. He is **Pte. W. Altree**, who before enlisting lived with his mother at West Thebarton, Australia. He enlisted in November, and after a short period in Egypt proceeded to the Peninsula. He was a native of Bolton, and in his boyhood attended Oxford Grove Council School. He kept in touch with his fellow schoolboys and his name is on the role of honour at the school. He was 18 years of age and had been in Australia two years.

Bolton Journal and Guardian

Bolton Emigrant Killed

News has been received of the death at the Dardanelles of **Private William Altree** of the Australian contingent. Altree was well known in the Smithills district, where he lived at 36, Stanley-rd before emigrating to Adelaide two years ago. He had worked at the Haslam and Musgrave spinning mills, and latterly at the Atlas Furnishing Company, Knowsley-st., Bolton. He had been engaged in farming and was quite satisfied with Australian life. He was of a jovial disposition, and had made a wide circle of friends, by whom he is sadly missed.

William was the son of Albert Henry Altree b.1852, a brassfounder, and Clarissa Altree née Jopson b.1853.

He was one of ten children, two of whom had died by the 1911 Census.

William left Liverpool for Australia aboard the SS Irishman on 24 September 1913.

His occupation was given as shop assistant.

He was working as a labourer when he enlisted in the AIF in Oaklands, a suburb of Adelaide, South Australia on 9 December 1914.

His unit embarked from Melbourne, Australia on HMAT Runic on 19 February 1915. He was listed as unmarried and a labourer.

His address was 1 Murray Street, Thebarton, South Australia and his next of kin was listed as Mrs Clara Altree of the same address. He was paid 5 shillings a day.

His mother's address was given as 10 Northern Grove, Bolton.

He was described on his enlistment medical report as being 18 years 6 months old, 133 lbs, 5' 5½" tall with grey eyes, fair hair and a bright complexion. He had two vaccination marks on his right arm, a scar above his left wrist and two scars on his forehead. His religion was Congregationalist.

He had been a pupil at Oxford Grove Council School, Bolton and his name appears on the Roll of Honour displayed at the current school.

Name	Altree, William Truman
Rank	Private
Number	1452
Unit	10th Bn Australian Imperial Force
Born	Aspull, Wigan, Lancashire 1896
Enlisted	Oaklands, South Australia 9 December 1914
Died	Gallipoli, Turkey 29 May 1915
Age	19
Grave or Memorial	Shrapnel Valley Cemetery, Gallipoli, Turkey

Thomas Baines

Bolton Journal and Guardian

An excellent record for soldiering is that of a former Lostock Junction family, who are now living at Eccles. Mr W. Baines, landlord of the Fox Vaults, Eccles, has six out of seven sons with the Army. All are or have been in the Lancashire Fusiliers. Their names are John Baines, of the Connaught Rangers, a time-expired Lancashire Fusilier, who re-enlisted at the outbreak of the war; William Baines,also a time expired Lancashire Fusilier, now serving with the Army Medical Corps; George Baines,with the Lancashire Fusiliers at Barrow; **Tom Baines** of the 1st Lancashire Fusiliers; Sergt. J. Baines, 2nd Lancashire Fusiliers. At Lostock Junction the father carried on the business of a market gardener. All the sons are well known in the Lostock and Westhoughton district. Tom Baines is reported to have been killed in action in the Gallipoli Peninsular on the 11th May, and Richard is at a field hospital in France suffering from gas poisoning. Sergt James Baines was wounded early in the fighting in France, but is now back in the fighting line.

Thomas was the son of William Baines b.1856, a nurseryman / gardener, and Ann Baines née Bannister b.1856.

In 1891 Thomas was living at 160 Chew Moor Lane, Lostock, Bolton with his parents and siblings John b.1876, William b.1875, Margaret (Maggie) b.1880, Barnaby b.1882, George b.1885 and James b.1889.

The 1901 Census listed Thomas as living at Lostock Park Nursery, Wingates with his parents and siblings Margaret, Barnaby, George, James and Richard b.1892.

Thomas was employed as a piecer in a cotton mill.

Name	Baines, Thomas
Rank	Private
Number	1338
Unit	1st Bn Lancashire Fusiliers
Born	Aspull, Lancashire c.1886
Enlisted	Bury, Lancashire
Died	Gallipoli, Turkey 25 April 1915
Age	28
Grave or Memorial	Helles Memorial Gallipoli, Turkey

Name	Barlow, Samuel
Rank	Private
Number	17789
Unit	1st Bn Border Regiment
Born	Rotherham, Yorkshire 1895
Enlisted	Bury, Lancashire September 1914
Died	Gallipoli, Turkey 21 December 1915
Age	20
Grave or Memorial	Lancashire Landing Cemetery, Gallipoli, Turkey

Samuel Barlow

Samuel was the son of Richard Barlow b.1866, a labourer in an ironworks and previously a coal miner, and Mary Alice Barlow née Worthington b.1868.

Samuel first appeared on the Census in 1901, living at 26 Rose Hill Road, Rawmarsh, Rotherham, Yorkshire along with his parents and siblings Alma b.1891, Albert b.1893, William b.1898 and Nora b.1900.

Richard and Mary Alice were born in Bolton and they had returned there by 1904.

By 1911 Samuel was living at 17 Romer Street, Tong Fold, Bolton with his parents and siblings Alma, Albert, William, Nora, Nellie b.1902, Nancy b.1904, Sidney b.1906, Thomas b.1908 and Nelson b.1910.

Samuel was working as a plaiter down in a bleachworks.

On enlistment he gave his previous employment as being a starcher.

His Army medical examination recorded him as being 5' 5 1/2" tall and weighing 112 lbs with a fresh complexion, blue eyes and brown hair.

William Barlow

Bolton Journal and Guardian 24 November 1916

Pte. WILLIAM BARLOW, L.N.L. Regiment was formerly reported missing since August 10th, 1915, and the Army Council have now decided that he died on that date. Another old boy of St. Thomas's School, Halliwell, he was formerly in the King's Liverpool Regiment, and his parents live at 94 Darley-st., Halliwell. His brother Edward is also on active Service.

William was the son of John Barlow b.1856, a brickworks labourer, and Orpha Helen (Ellen) Barlow née Brooks b.1862.

William first appeared on the 1891 Census living at 137 Darley Street, Bolton with his parents, brother Albert b.1889 and grandmother Mary Brooks.

William's mother died in 1896. His father remarried to Mary Chesworth in 1899.

On the 1901 Census William was living at 94 Darley Street with his father, step-mother and brothers Albert, James b.1894, Ernest b.1896 and John b.1901.

William was working in the card room of a cotton mill.

In 1911 William was living at the same address with his father, step-mother and brothers Albert, James and Ernest.

At the time William was working for the Corporation Street Department and is listed as being single*.

The brother Edward referred to in the Journal article appears to be a misprint.

According to his medical examination on enlisting, William was 5' 6 1/8" tall and weighed 159 lbs with brown eyes, dark brown hair and a fresh complexion. He also had a tattoo of Baden Powell (either the words or a picture) on his right forearm.

His occupation at the time was given as carter.

* *His Army enlistment papers record him as having married Jane Cooke in Bolton on 16 July 1904 and having had three children: Eva b.1906, Lily b.1908 and Sarah Ann b.1909 - however the names are all crossed out on the document. This appears to have been a clerical error, confusing him with another William Barlow of a similar age who did fit that description and lived at 3 Reservoir Street, Bolton.*

Name
Barlow, William
Rank
Private
Number
13515
Unit
6th Bn The Loyal North Lancashire Regiment
Born
Bolton, Lancashire 1884
Enlisted
Bolton, Lancashire 31 August 1914
Died
Gallipoli, Turkey 10 August 1915
Age
31
Grave or Memorial
Helles Memorial, Gallipoli, Turkey

Name
Beardsworth, Arthur
Rank
Private
Number
Deal/3776(S)
Unit
Royal Marines Hood Battalion (Royal Marines Medical Unit attached Hood Battalion), Royal Naval Division
Born
Bolton, Lancashire 1897
Enlisted
7 April 1915
Died
Gallipoli, Turkey 26 December 1915
Age
18
Grave or Memorial
Skew Bridge Cemetery, Helles, Gallipoli, Turkey

Arthur Beardsworth

Bolton Journal and Guardian 28 January 1916

Youthful Ambulance Man Killed

The parents of **Pte. Arthur Beardsworth**, who lives at 35, Darley-st., S3776 Medical Unit, 1st Field Ambulance, Royal Naval Division, have received an official notification of his death at the Dardanelles on December 26th. He was only 18 years of age last August, and was called up through the St John Ambulance Brigade and was drafted to Blandford, where, after six months' training he went to the Dardanelles. He was formerly a member of the Bolton Lads' Club, where he was held in high esteem. For the last eight or nine years he had been connected with the Raphael-st Mission, where his name is on the Roll of Honour. His name also appears on the Rolls of Honour at the Hanover Chapel, Gilnow-rd. and Brownlow Fold Council School. He was employed as a piecer at the Musgrave Spinning Company's No. 6 Mill.

Bolton Journal and Guardian

Mrs. Beardsworth, 35, Darley-st., Brownlow Fold, has given three sons to His Majesty's service, and a few weeks ago we had the sad duty of chronicling the death of one, the youngest of the three, **Arthur** being killed whilst serving in the Royal Naval Division Medical Unit. Another son, William Henry, enlisted on Sept. 23rd, in the King's Royal Rifle (Church Lad's Brigade), and after training at Denham, Clipstone Park Camp, and Salisbury went on foreign service on November 5th, 1915. Albert, the eldest, on November 23rd, 1914, joined the Royal Naval Division Medical Unit, and after being in training at Blandford left for foreign service on February 16th of this year, going to Mudros. All three are old scholars of Brownlow Fold Council School as well as members of the Independent Order of Rechabites*, Salford Unity, Primrose Tent.

Arthur was the son of John William Beardsworth b.1869, a joiner, and Clara Beardsworth née Greenwood B.1869.

On the 1911 Census the family were living at 35 Darley Street, Brownlow Fold, Bolton.

Arthur was listed as a piecer in a cotton mill.

He had 2 older brothers - Albert b.1895 and William Henry b.1896, who both worked as piecers.

He also had a younger brother - Robert b.1902 and 2 younger sisters - Edith Annie b.1903 and Clara b.1906.

* A temperance-based friendly society

Thomas Belsey

Bolton Journal and Guardian

Pte. H. BELSEY, L.N. L. Regt., is suffering from gunshot wounds in the knee received on October 27th. He lives at 26, Emmanuel-st., Bolton, and was employed at Messrs. Magee, Marshall and Co.'s Brewery. His two brothers, Stephen and **Thomas**, have been killed.

Thomas was the son of Henry Belsey b.1859, who worked as a labourer (with Bolton Corporation Street Department by 1911) and Rachel Belsey née Brown b.1863.

In the 1891 Census Thomas and his parents were living in Runcorn, Cheshire with their 3 other children - Mary Ann b.1883, Stephen John b.1886 and Sarah Jane b.1890.

By 1901 Thomas and the family had relocated to Bolton and were living at 22 Oak Street, Bolton with Mary Ann, Stephen John (both then working in cotton mills), Sarah Jane, Susan b.1893 and George Henry b.1896.

On the 1911 Census Thomas was listed as serving as a Private with 1st Bn Lancashire Fusiliers in Multan, Punjab, India.

Back in Bolton Henry and Rachel Belsey were still listed as living at 22 Oak Street with (George) Henry and grandson Alfred Belsey b.1903. Two out of seven of their children were listed as having died by 1911.

Stephen John Belsey enlisted in the Militia at Bury as part of the Lancashire Fusiliers in early 1904 before joining the Regiment proper in August 1904. In 1911 he is listed as overseas military personnel as a Private with 1st Bn South Lancashire Regiment at Napier Barracks, Lahore, India. His death in WW1, mentioned in the article above (if correct), does not appear to have been recorded.

Name
Belsey, Thomas
Rank
Private
Number
1254
Unit
1st Bn Lancashire Fusiliers
Born
Warrington, Lancashire 1887
Enlisted
Bury, Lancashire
Died
Gallipoli, Turkey 25 April 1915
Age
27
Grave or Memorial
Helles Memorial, Gallipoli, Turkey

James Bamford Bennett

Bolton Journal and Guardian 28 May 1915

A HORWICH FAMILY'S RECORD

Bolton and district has played a notable part in helping to swell the ranks of the Army, and large numbers of families have several members to the colours. Mr. John Bennett, a boiler maker at the Horwich loco. Works, who lives in Alexandra-rd., has five sons, three sons-in-law, and a grandson serving. One son, **Private James B. Bennett**, has been killed in action in the Dardanelles. Private Bennett had been in the Army for some years, and for four years prior to January was stationed in India, when he came home with his regiment. He was unmarried, and formerly worked in the Victoria Mill. Mr Bennett now has four sons in the Army as follows: Pte. Joshua Bennett, 2nd Manchester Regiment, who joined seven years ago, was for a considerable time in France, and is now recuperating in this country, having been wounded at Ypres. Driver W. Bennett, Royal Garrison Artillery (Heavy Brigade), now in France, is a reservist, who was called up at the outbreak of war, having had seven years' previous service in the Army. He has also been to India. He formerly resided in Dale-st., Horwich, with his wife and two children. Pte. John Bennett is attached to the Royal Lancaster Regiment. He is a married man with three children. The youngest member of the family, Robt. Bennett, joined the 12th Battalion Lancashire Fusiliers in September, and is now stationed at Seaford. Mr. Bennett's eldest son, Thomas, is also actively engaged at Messrs. Cammell Laird and Company's works at Birkenhead, on Government work. Private Joshua Bennett, a son of Private Joshua Bennett, and a grandson of Mr. Bennett senr., is at present in Egypt with the Manchester Territorials. Mr. Bennett has also three sons-in-law in the Army, the husbands of his three daughters - Private Wm. Laithwaite, Pals' Battalion of the 5th Loyal North Lancashire Regiment; Private Thomas Whittle, County Palatine Royal Engineers; and Private Benjamin Alton, Manchester Pals.

James was the son of John Bennett b.1851, a boiler maker at Horwich Loco Works, and Christiana Bennett née Alton b.1853.

On the 1891 Census he was living at 47 Summer Street, Horwich with his parents and siblings Thomas b.1876, Joshua b.1878, Mary Jane b.1880, William b.1881, John b.1883, Christiana b.1885 and Elizabeth b.1888.

His mother died in 1898 and at the time of the 1901 Census James was living at 5 Travers Street, Horwich with his father and sisters Christiana and Elizabeth (Ann) and brothers John and Robert b.1893.

By the 1911 Census James was serving abroad in the Army and his father was living at 2 Alexandra Road, Lostock with children Elizabeth Ann, Robert and daughter Mary Jane, her husband Thomas Whittle and their daughter Susannah b.1901.

James was the uncle of Private Joshua Bennett who was killed in action at Gallipoli on 19 June 1915 while serving with 1st/9th Bn Manchester Regiment.

Name	
Bennett, James Bamford	
Rank	
Private	
Number	
2200	
Unit	
1st Bn Lancashire Fusiliers	
Born	
Horwich, Lancashire 1890	
Enlisted	
Bury, Lancashire	
Died	
Gallipoli, Turkey 25 April 1915	
Age	
25	
Grave or Memorial	
Helles Memorial, Gallipoli, Turkey	

Joshua Bennett

Bolton Journal and Guardian 28 May 1915

A HORWICH FAMILY'S RECORD

Bolton and district has played a notable part in helping to swell the ranks of the Army, and large numbers of families have several members to the colours. Mr John Bennett, a boiler maker at the Horwich loco. Works, who lives in Alexandra-rd., has five sons, three sons-in-law, and a grandson serving. One son, Private James B. Bennett, has been killed in action in the Dardanelles. Private Bennett had been in the Army for some years, and for four years prior to January was stationed in India, when he came home with his regiment. He was unmarried, and formerly worked in the Victoria Mill. Mr. Bennett now has four sons in the Army as follows: Pte. Joshua Bennett, 2nd Manchester Regiment, who joined seven years ago, was for a considerable time in France, and is now recuperating in this country, having been wounded at Ypres. Driver W. Bennett, Royal Garrison Artillery (Heavy Brigade), now in France, is a reservist, who was called up at the outbreak of war, having had seven years' previous service in the Army. He has also been to India. He formerly resided in Dale-st., Horwich, with his wife and two children. Pte. John Bennett is attached to the Royal Lancaster Regiment. He is a married man with three children. The youngest member of the family, Robt. Bennett, joined the 12th Battalion Lancashire Fusiliers in September, and is now stationed at Seaford. Mr. Bennett's eldest son, Thomas, is also actively engaged at Messrs. Cammell Laird and Company's works at Birkenhead, on Government work. **Private Joshua Bennett**, a son of Private Joshua Bennett, and a grandson of Mr. Bennett senr., is at present in Egypt with the Manchester Territorials. Mr. Bennett has also three sons-in-law in the Army, the husbands of his three daughters - Private Wm. Laithwaite, Pals' Battalion of the 5th Loyal North Lancashire Regiment; Private Thomas Whittle, County Palatine Royal Engineers; and Private Benjamin Alton, Manchester Pals.

Joshua was the son of Joshua Bennett b.1878, variously a blacksmith's striker and a holder up for a boiler maker, and Annie Bennett née Whittle b.1877.

On the 1901 Census he was living at 47 Raglan Street, Preston, Lancashire with his parents, sister Mary Jane b.1899 and brother Albert b.1901.

By the 1911 Census the family were living at 72 Brook Street, Ashton-Under-Lyne and had three more children, Amelia b.1903, John b.1906 and Elizabeth b.1908.

Joshua was the nephew of Private James Bamford Bennett who was killed in action at Gallipoli on 25 April 1915 while serving with 1st Bn Lancashire Fusiliers.

Name	
	Bennett, Joshua
Rank	
	Private
Number	
	1740
Unit	
	1st/9th Bn Manchester Regiment
Born	
	Horwich, Lancashire 1896
Enlisted	
	Ashton-Under-Lyne, Lancashire
Died	
	Gallipoli, Turkey 19 June 1915
Age	
	19
Grave or Memorial	
	Helles Memorial, Gallipoli, Turkey

John Birch

Bolton Journal and Guardian 21 May 1915

Local Soldiers Killed in the Dardanelles

Private John Birch, of the first Battalion Lancashire Fusiliers, was Killed on May 11th, five days after his 30th birthday. Birch, whose parents live at 37 Windley-st., had been in the Army nearly seven years, and when hostilities broke out his regiment was at Aden. They came to Nuneaton, however, and then went out with the Dardanelles land force. His brother, Peter Birch, has been in the Navy about three years, and since the commencement of the war has steamed about 30,000 miles in H.M.S. Defence. He is 23 years of age. Their father formerly saw service with the Bolton Artillery Territorials.

John was the son of John Birch, an iron moulder, b.1864 and Martha Jane Birch née Nuttall b.1863.

On the 1891 Census John and his parents were listed with his siblings, Mary Alice b.1867 and William b.1889. Martha Jane's widowed mother Emma Nuttall was also living with them.

On the 1901 Census young John was working as a piecer in a cotton mill. Son William was no longer present but three more children were listed - Peter b.1892, Annie b.1899 and Ellen b.1901. Martha's mother had been joined in the house by John Birch Snr's widowed father William Birch.

By the 1911 Census John was serving as a Private with 1st Bn Lancashire Fusiliers in Multan, Punjab, India.

His parents were living at 37 Windley Street with Peter and Annie. Children William, Ellen and one other unknown child had died by this point and the in-laws were no longer present. Mary Alice was resident with her husband Samuel Entwistle and their daughter, Ellen Entwistle.

John's brother, Stoker Peter Birch, was killed at the Battle of Jutland with the loss of his ship, HMS Defence, on 31 May 1916.

Jack Blackburn

AIF Witness statements:

Pte T E Foley 1 September 1917

On the 25th April 1915 I was with **Pte Blackburn** just about Johnsons Jolly at Gallipoli at dusk in the evening. The pltn that we were with had to retire a little. As we retired out of the little trench we had made, Pte Blackburn was hit and fell. I did not see him after this but I was told by one of our party that Pte Blackburn was shot through the head. I cannot remember the man who told me this. By the way that Pte Blackburn fell and lay I was sure that he was shot dead.

L/Sgt C P Stephen 12 January 1916

Witness says **Blackburn** was in his section. They were both at the landing on 25.4.15. The last witness saw of Blackburn was on the Monday afternoon about 4.30 during an advance. Soon afterwards they had to retire under very heavy fire and lost a number of men.

Jack was the son of William Blackburn b.1863 and Fanny Rachel Blackburn née Ince b.1866.

He had at least two brothers, Joseph b.1887 and Thomas Carr Blackburn b.1890 (died the same year).

William Blackburn probably died in 1892. Fanny Rachel Blackburn died in 1895.

Jack first appeared on the 1901 Census as an inmate of Eden's Orphanage, Astley Bridge, Bolton along with his brother Joseph.

By 1911 he was living at Pendlebury's Farm, Smithills, Bolton with his employer James Taylor, his wife and their son. Jack was working on the farm as a labourer.

At some point between 1911 and 1914 he emigrated to Australia where he worked as a labourer.

His medical examination on enlistment recorded him as being 5' 6 3/8" tall and weighing 9 st with a dark complexion, Blue eyes and dark brown hair. He also had a scar on his lower lip.

He left Melbourne, Australia on board HMAT Hororata on 19 October 1914.

His brother Joseph, who was given as next of kin on Jack's Army records, lived for a while at Emmanuel College, Saskatchewan, Canada but by 1917 was back in England, living in Ramsgate, Kent.

Name
Blackburn, Jack
Rank
Private
Number
597
Unit
7th Bn Australian Imperial Force
Born
Horwich/Rivington, Lancashire 1892
Enlisted
Geelong, Victoria, Australia 9 September 1914
Died
Gallipoli, Turkey 25 April 1915
Age
23
Grave or Memorial
Lone Pine Memorial, Gallipoli, Turkey

Thomas Blackledge

Bolton Journal and Guardian 21 May 1915

Local Soldiers Killed in the Dardanelles

The War Office has also conveyed the news to Mrs. Blackledge, 8, Benson-st., Smithills, that her son, **Private Thomas Blackledge**, who was serving with A Company, 1st Battalion, Lancashire Fusiliers, was recently killed in the operations at the Dardanelles. He had been stationed several years at Karachi, India, coming to England at the beginning of the year, when he was granted a furlough. In a letter recently received by his mother, Private Blackledge stated that he was in the best of health, but by the time she would receive the letter he would be in the thick of the fighting. Much sympathy is felt with Mrs. Blackledge, whose husband and four other sons are serving with the Army. Blackledge was formerly connected with St. Joseph's R.C. School, and when on furlough at New Year's time he tendered his thanks to Mr. W. H. Hall, secretary of St. Joseph's Confraternity, for the many welcome letters he received when he was in India.

Thomas was the son of Miles William Blackledge, a railway carter, b.1865 and Maria Blackledge née Townsend b.1863.

On the 1901 Census Thomas was listed as living at 8 Benson Street, Bolton with his parents and two older brothers John b.1888 and Daniel b.1891 and two younger brothers, Miles b.1895 and Robert b.1899.

By 1911 Thomas was serving in the Army.

On the 1911 Census the rest of the family were still at 8 Benson Street in 1911 and there was also another son, Joseph b.1904.

Miles William Blackledge served with the Royal Field Artillery in France during the First World War.

Miles Blackledge was killed in action on the Western Front on 31 July 1917 while serving with 1st/4th Bn The Loyal North Lancashire Regiment.

Name	
Blackledge, Thomas	
Rank	
Private	
Number	
1888	
Unit	
1st Bn Lancashire Fusiliers	
Born	
Horwich, Lancashire c.1893	
Enlisted	
Bury, Lancashire	
Died	
Gallipoli, Turkey 25 April 1915	
Age	
22	
Grave or Memorial	
Helles Memorial, Gallipoli, Turkey	

Robert Hutchinson Booth

Bolton Journal and Guardian 7 January 1916

The Late Capt. Booth - Sad Loss to Turton

News of the death of **Captain Robert Hutchinson Booth**, of the Army Service Corps, and only son of Major Booth, V.D., J.P., of Turton, has created profound regret in the Bolton district, where he was widely known, and especially in Turton, where he resided at Horrobin Fold. A cable was received on Monday to the effect that Capt. Booth had succumbed at Cotonera Hospital. Malta, from pneumonia following a gun-shot wound. A later cable said the deceased was buried on January 2nd (the day of his death) in Pieta Cemetery, Malta. It was at first reported that he was in hospital with a fractured leg but unfortunately the real news revealed more serious circumstances. Joining the 4th battalion, East Lancashires, at Blackburn about ten years ago as a Territorial officer, he has had a useful career in military service. Five years ago he transferred to the Army Service Corps, and became an adjutant in Egypt shortly after the outbreak of the war. In Gallipoli he served as deputy-quartermaster-general to the 42nd East Lancashire Division, and aide-de-camp to General Douglas, and shore commandant at Cape Helles.

He was 32 years old, married, and connected with Wellington Mills, Turton, and Messrs. Booth's business at Ashton, and had management of the doubling section. His wife was formerly Miss Monk, daughter of the late Mr. A. Monk, jeweller, of Bolton, and she and her baby son, together with Major and Mrs. Booth are the recipients of much sincere sympathy.

Capt. Booth had many interests apart from his business and military connexions. He was connected with the Turton Conservative Club, took a lively interest in amateur theatricals, and was a sidesman at Turton Church. He was a sportsman of considerable attainments, an excellent tennis and good golf player, and he had twice won the President's Cup at the Turton Golf Club. He was also a member of the Holcombe Hunt, and a splendid horseman. His death will create a void in the village which will be keenly felt and exceedingly difficult to fill.

At a special meeting of the County magistrates, yesterday, deep sympathy was expressed with Major Booth in the loss of his son. The Clerk (Mr. A. Tyldsley) was instructed to forward a letter of condolence to Major Booth and family.

Robert was the son of John Booth, Master Cotton Spinner, b.1854 and Mary Agnes Booth née Taylor b.1858.

On the 1891 Census John was listed as living at Lynwood, Station Road, Turton with his parents, his sister Margaret b.1889 and a Governess and a servant.

By 1901 the family had moved to Hazel Bank, Turton and had two servants. Robert's occupation was given as Apprentice Master Cotton Spinner, presumably working for his father.

In 1911 the family were still at Hazel Bank. Robert's occupation was given as Master Doubler.

He was commissioned as a 2nd Lieutenant in the 1st Volunteer Bn Lancashire Fusiliers in 1905 and became a Lieutenant in 1908. He moved to the East Lancashire Company of the Army Service Corps in 1910.

He married Elsie Mary Monk at St Anne's Church, Turton in 1913 and they had one son Robert Arthur Booth b.1915. Robert left effects of £1172 7s to his widow. His son, Robert Arthur Booth, died in 1943 while serving as a Lieutenant with the Middlesex Regiment.

Name
Booth, Robert Hutchinson
Rank
Captain
Unit
Army Service Corps 42nd East Lancs Field Ambulance
Born
Turton, Lancashire c.1883
Died
Cottonera Military Hospital, Malta 1 January 1916
Age
32
Grave or Memorial
Pieta Military Cemetery, Malta

Name	
Brittain, William	
Rank	
Lance Corporal	
Number	
9849	
Unit	
1st Bn	
Border Regiment	
Born	
Leitrim, Ireland	
c.1892	
Enlisted	
Manchester	
Died	
Gallipoli, Turkey	
28 April 1915	
Age	
23	
Grave or Memorial	
Helles Memorial,	
Gallipoli, Turkey	

William Brittain

Bolton Journal and Guardian

IN THE DARDANELLES

Official news has been received by the parents of **Lance-Sergeant Wm. Brittain** (9849), who lived at 7, Curzon-rd, that he was killed in the Dardanelles on May 14th. He was attached to the 1st Border Regiment and has served in the Army for the past six years, the last two of which have been in India. He was 23 years of age.

William was the son of James Brittain b.1872, a grave digger, and Mary Alice Brittain b.1876. The family had moved to Bolton from Leinster in Ireland in the late 1890s.

On the 1901 Census William was living at 56 Balshaw Street, Bolton with his parents and sisters Eliza Jane b.1895 and Fanny Ann b.1898.

By 1911 William was serving in the Army and his parents were living at 21 Vincent Street, Bolton with Eliza Jane and sons John James b.1901 and Thomas Albert b.1903.

Fanny Ann Brittain had died in 1908 aged 10.

Richard Browitt

Richard was the son of Henry Browitt, a collier, b.1853 and Alice Browitt b.1856.

He married Margaret Delaney (b.1878) in Wigan in 1902 and the family moved to Bolton c.1910, appearing on the 1911 Census at 7 Holt Street, off Deane Road, Bolton.

On the the 1911 census they had 7 children, Annie b.1899, James b.1901, Richard b.1905, Gerald b.1906, Noah b.1908, Cornelius b.1909 and Arnold b.1911.

Another daughter, Nancy, was born in 1913.

He had worked as a Bessemer steel breaker before enlisting.

Name	Browitt, Richard
Rank	Corporal
Number	4738
Unit	1st Bn Lancashire Fusiliers
Born	Wigan, Lancashire 1876
Enlisted	Bury, Lancashire
Died	Gallipoli, Turkey 21 August 1915
Age	39
Grave or Memorial	Helles Memorial, Gallipoli, Turkey

Name	
Bunce, Frederick Robert	
Rank	
Junior Reserve Attendant	
Number	
M/9823	
Unit	
Portsmouth Bn	
Royal Naval Division,	
Royal Naval Auxiliary	
Sick Berth Reserve	
Born	
Leamington	
Spa, Warwickshire	
14 June 1884	
Enlisted	
9 August 1914	
Died	
At sea	
14 May 1915	
Age	
30	
Grave or Memorial	
Cairo War Memorial	
Cemetery,	
Egypt	

Frederick Robert Bunce

Farnworth Weekly Journal 28 May 1915

AMBULANCE MAN KILLED

Lance-Corporal Fred. R. Bunce of 50 Georgiana-st., whose death with the Royal Marine Light Infantry at the Dardanelles we recorded last week, was a native of Leamington, and came to Farnworth some 16 years ago when he secured a situation as porter at Farnworth Station, and lived with Mr. W. Freeman. He went to Bolton when the erection of the new Trinity-st Station was begun, and has recently been night foreman porter there, varying the work in summers by serving the L. and Y. Railway as ticket collector at Blackpool. He was married about four years ago to Miss Martha Hall, who worked for Mr. W. Sumner, J.P., and was connected with Holland's School, and they had one child, a little girl. His own school was the Market-st Wesleyans, at which he used to be a very regular attender. He was a keen ambulance man, and took part with the railway team in several competitions, for success in which he holds certificates and a medal. When the war broke out he was attached to the Royal Naval Sick Berth Reserve, but was transferred to the Royal Marine Light Infantry field ambulance. His duties brought him into the trenches during the siege of Antwerp, where he came under fire whilst conveying the wounded to hospital, but before that he had been at Chatham helping with the hospital train, as also at Ostend. Fifteen weeks ago he went to Egypt with the Plymouth Battalion, and it was from there that he found his way to the Dardanelles, where he was injured on May 11th, dying from his wounds on the 17th.* All who knew him regret the loss of one who was so useful and highly respected. The staff of Trinity-st Station met on Friday, under the chairmanship of the stationmaster, Mr. Firth, and passed a vote of condolence with the widow, whilst on Sunday the Rev. Bramwell Brown made appropriate reference to his loss from the pulpit of Wesley Chapel. On Sunday afternoon Mr. T. Lawton announced his demise from the platform of Wesley School and testified to the consistent life he had led, asking the scholars to remember his widow and child in their prayers, and the hymn "The Homeland" was sung. Lance-Corpl. Bunce has two brothers serving with the colours, one in France and the other in training in Leamington.

Frederick was the son of John William Bunce b.1851, a carrier, and Ann Bunce née Baldwin b.1856.

He first appeared on the 1891 Census living in the village of Nightcote, Burton Dassett, Warwickshire with his parents and brothers George H b.1888 and Alfred b1890.

By 1901 he was living at 38 Darley Grove, Farnworth with his uncle and aunt, William and Emily Freeman and their three daughters. He was employed as a railway porter.

Frederick married Martha Hall b.1884 at Farnworth Wesleyan Chapel, Egerton Street, Moses Gate in 1911.

In 1911 the couple were living at 50 Georgiana Street, Farnworth.

They had one daughter, Annie b.1912.

Frederick's service records list him as being 5' 11" tall with a fresh complexion, blue eyes and brown hair.

His name is on Farnworth War Memorial and the Lancashire and Yorkshire Railway War Memorial on Victoria Station, Manchester.

* Actually died on 14th May 1915 as per CWGC who also give his unit as Portsmouth Bn.

Thomas Helme Byrne

Bolton Journal and Guardian 15 October 1915

Missing in Gallipoli

Word has been received by Mr. J. Helm 3, Lydgate, Breightmet, that **Pte. Thomas Helm Byrne**, whom he adopted, is reported missing after an engagement in Gallipoli on August 9th. This adds another name to the long list of casualties published in connexion with the 6th Loyal North Lancashire Regiment in their charge at at the new landings in Suvla Bay. Pte. Byrne, who was a signaller, and 19 years of age, enlisted on August 17th last year, and after being in training at Preston, Tidworth, Aldershot and Blackdown,he proceeded to the Dardanelles. Prior to enlisting he resided in Tonge Moor. He was employed at the Tootill Bridge Bleachworks. His name is on the St. Augustine's Roll of Honour.

Thomas was the son of Clara Byrne.

On the 1911 Census he was listed as Thomas Helme Byrne - the adopted son of John and Jane Helme of 37 Stone Street, Bolton.

Thomas worked as an apprentice sawyer in a saw mill. John Helme was a joiner at a bleachworks and Jane was a housewife.

Name
Byrne, Thomas Helme
Rank
Private
Number
11401
Unit
6th Bn The Loyal North Lancashire Regiment
Born
Bolton, Lancashire 1896
Enlisted
Bolton, Lancashire 17 August 1914
Died
Gallipoli, Turkey 9 August 1915
Age
19
Grave or Memorial
Helles Memorial, Gallipoli, Turkey

William Shepherd Calderley

Journal and Guardian 10 September 1915

MISSING IN GALLIPOLI

In an engagement on the Gallipoli Peninsula on August 9th, the 6th Battalion Loyal North Lancashire Regiment, seems to have suffered heavily, a number of casualties to Bolton soldiers in that unit having been reported. Mr. Calderley, of 64, Victoria-grove, has received official intimation that his son, **Pte. William Calderley** (12882), 6th L.N.L., has been missing since the engagement referred to. Calderley, who is only 18 years of age, enlisted soon after the outbreak of war, and went out to join the Mediterranean Expeditionary Force in June. Prior to enlisting he was employed at Messrs. Murton's bleachworks, Astley Bridge, and was connected with Park-st. Wesleyan Sunday School. His younger brother, Pte. Robert Calderley, is at Aldershot with the 9th L.N.L.

Bolton Journal and Guardian

Mr. and Mrs. Calderley, 4 Osborne-grove, Bolton, have been informed that their son, **Pte. WILIAM CALDERLEY**, L.N.L. Regt., who had been missing in Gallipoli since Aug. 9th, 1915, is now presumed to have died on that date. Aged 20 he was employed at Messrs. Murton's bleachworks, Astley Bridge, before enlisting in the month War broke out. His name is on the Roll of Honour at Oxford-grove Council School and Park-st. Wesleyan Church.

William was the son of William Calderley b.1863, a moulder's crane drive in an iron foundry and Ann Calderley née Holt b.1865.

On the 1911 Census their address was 64 Victoria Grove, Bolton.

William was the brother of Joseph b.1890, Harry b.1891, Robert b.1893 (see below) Annie b.18995, Bessie b.1902, Harold b.1907 and Stanley b.1909. His older brothers all worked as piecers in a cotton mill in 1911.

William's cousin, Joseph Calderley, was killed in the same battle at Chunuk Bair, Gallipoli on the same day as William, 9 August 1915.

William's brother, Private Robert Calderley was killed in action in France on 1 September 1914.

Name	Calderley, William Shepherd
Rank	Private
Number	12882
Unit	6th Bn The Loyal North Lancashire Regiment
Born	Bolton, Lancashire 1896
Enlisted	Bolton, Lancashire
Died	Gallipoli, Turkey 9 August 1915
Age	19
Grave or Memorial	Helles Memorial, Gallipoli, Turkey

Joseph Calderley

Bolton Journal and Guardian 8 December 1916

Pte. JOS. CALDERLEY, Loyal North Lancashire Regt., is officially reported to have perished in Gallipoli, although nothing definite as to his actual fate has been heard since August, 1915, when he was posted as missing. Previous to enlisting at the outbreak of war, he resided with his mother at 36, Reservoir-st., Bolton, and worked at Messrs. Walmsley's forge. Aged 23 he is on the Rolls of Honour at Christ Church and St. Mark's.

Joseph was the son of Henry Calderley b.1858, a brick maker, and Ellen Calderley née Worthington b.1857.

Henry and Ellen appeared on the 1881 Census living with their cousin's family at 1 Whittaker Street, Bolton.

On the 1891 census Ellen was living (without Henry) at 1 Adam Street, Bolton with daughters Hannah b.1882, Ellen b.1886 and May b.1889.

On the 1901 Census Ellen was listed as widowed and living at 75 Commission Street, Bolton with daughters Hannah, Ellen, Margaret Ann (May) and son Thomas b.1895.

Joseph first appeared in the 1901 Census as the adopted son of John and Ann Gregory of 36 Reservoir Street, Bolton and again at the same address in 1911 as the adopted son of either Mark Gregory (John and Ann's son) or Mary Ellen Bromley (their daughter) and her husband George Bromley.

In 1911 Joseph was employed as a forge hand (castings filer) in an iron works.

Joseph's actual mother, Ellen, lived until 1925 and wrote to the Army asking for information about her son when he was posted as missing at Gallipoli.

At his Army medical examination Joseph Calderley was recorded as being 5' 3 1/8" tall and having a fair/pale complexion, grey eyes and light brown hair. He was tattooed with "several dots" on his forearm.

Joseph's cousin, William Shepherd Calderley, was killed in the same battle at Chunuk Bair, Gallipoli on the same day, 9 August 1915.

Joseph's other cousin (William's brother), Pte Robert Calderley, was killed in action in France on 1 September 1914.

Name	
Calderley, Joseph	
Rank	
Private	
Number	
12094	
Unit	
6th Bn The Loyal North Lancashire Regiment	
Born	
Bolton, Lancashire 1892	
Enlisted	
Bolton, Lancashire 27 August 1914	
Died	
Gallipoli, Turkey 9 August 1915	
Age	
23	
Grave or Memorial	
Helles Memorial, Gallipoli, Turkey	

Reuben Caldwell

Bolton Journal and Guardian 27 August 1915

Wingates Soldier Killed in the Dardanelles

Official information has been received by Mr. Caldwell, 4, Manchester Road, Wingates, that his son, **Private Reuben Caldwell** (3793) Connaught Rangers, has been killed in the Dardanelles. Pte. Caldwell, who enlisted in January, was drafted to the Dardanelles five or six weeks ago. Prior to enlisting he was employed at the Hulton Collieries. He is a married man, and resided at Croft-st., Wingates, and leaves a widow and two children.

Reuben was born Reuben Lonsdale, the son of Jane Lonsdale b.1868.

Jane Lonsdale married Reuben Caldwell b.1865, a coal miner/hewer, in 1890. It seems likely that Reuben Caldwell was his father.

On the 1891 Census, Reuben was listed as Reuben Lonsdale and living with his parents at 1 Thomas Street, Westhoughton along with sister Jane Caldwell b.1891.

In 1901 he was living with his parents at 2 Manchester Road, Westhoughton as Reuben Lonsdale Caldwell, along with his siblings Jane, Alice b.1893, Hannah b.1895 and Benjamin b.1900.

By the 1911 Census he was listed as Reuben Lonsdale again (Caldwell having been crossed out) and was described as a 'step son' and working as a below ground drawer of coal in a colliery. He was living at 4 Manchester Road, Wingates, Westhoughton with his parents and siblings Hannah, Benjamin, Thomas b.1903 and Elias b.1905.

As Reuben Lonsdale Caldwell he married Lucy Warren in Bolton in 1911.

They had two children, Ada b.1912 and Jesse b.1914.

His name is on Westhoughton War Memorial.

Name	
Caldwell, Reuben	
Rank	
Private	
Number	
3793	
Unit	
5th Bn Connaught Rangers	
Born	
Bolton, Lancashire 1888	
Enlisted	
Hindley, Lancashire	
Died	
Gallipoli, Turkey 10 August 1915	
Age	
27	
Grave or Memorial	
Helles Memorial, Gallipoli, Turkey	

Alfred Carey

Alfred was the son of John Thomas Carey b.1865, a blacksmith, and Maria Carey née Heaviside b.1863.

Alfred first appeared on the 1901 Census living at 6 St George's Court, Bolton with his parents and siblings John b.1888, William Stewart b.1893, Emily b.1898 and Bertha b.1900.

In 1911 he was living at 8 Gleave Street, Bolton with his parents and siblings William Stewart, Emily, Bertha, Arthur Stanley b.1902 and Lena b.1905.

Alfred was working as a scutcher in a bleachworks.

Name	Carey, Alfred
Rank	Corporal
Number	2404
Unit	1st Bn Lancashire Fusiliers
Born	Bolton, Lancashire 1895
Enlisted	Bury, Lancashire
Died	Egypt? 5 July 1915
Age	20
Grave or Memorial	Alexandria (Chatby) Military and War Memorial Cemetery Alexandria, Egypt

LEST WE FORGET

IN VNDYING MEMORY OF THE MEN
AND WOMEN OF BOLTON WHO GAVE
THEIR LIVES IN THE GREAT WAR
1914 - 1919

1914 - 1919

1939 - 1945

1939 - 1945

Alfred Carrington

Alfred's name appears on the Bolton Borough Roll of Honour.

Bolton's War Memorial in front of the Town Hall on Victoria Square was unveiled (without the now familiar flanking statues) by the **Earl of Derby** on 4 July 1928, the main ceremonial stone having been laid by **Sir Thomas Evans Flitcroft** (Mayor of Bolton 1926-27) on Armistice Day, 11 November 1927.

On the same afternoon the Bishop of Manchester dedicated the Hall of Remembrance in the portico of the Town Hall, directly facing the Cenotaph. It was financed by public subscription and is open to the public by prior arrangement.

The focus of the Hall of Remembrance is the Roll of Honour in the form of an illuminated vellum book, kept under glass, containing the names of over 3,500 men and women who lost their lives under arms or as civilian casualties during the First World War.

The criteria for inclusion used by the committee entrusted with compiling the Roll of Honour were:

"...to contain the names of those ordinarily resident in Bolton at the time of their enlistment, or were natives of the Borough and who fell in the Great War. Also any other exceptional cases to be considered on their merits."

The bronze figures on either side of the Cenotaph - the left representing "Peace Restraining War" and the right "Peace seeing the Horrors of War" - were finally unveiled on Armistice Day 1932.

These themes were controversial at the time and a long way in sentiment from the triumphalism of many other war memorials of the period.

The sculptor was **Walter Marsden**, an Accrington man (and holder of the Military Cross and Bar) who had himself fought alongside many Boltonians at Ypres and Cambrai as a 2nd Lieutenant in the Loyal North Lancashire Regiment during the First World War.

He created several other exceptional war memorials in Lancashire and his first hand experiences of the realities and suffering of war are reflected in the quiet dignity of his work.

Name
Carter, John Edwin

Rank
Corporal

Number
315

Unit
2nd/1st East Lancs Field Ambulance Royal Army Medical Corps

Born
Bolton, Lancashire 24 January 1893

Enlisted
Bolton, Lancashire

Died
At sea 13 August 1915

Age
22

Grave or Memorial
Helles Memorial, Gallipoli, Turkey

John Edwin Carter

John was the son of John Thomas Carter b.1856, a Corporation tramways labourer and earlier a railway porter and pointsman, and Hannah Maria Carter née Wade b.1864.

He first appeared on the 1901 Census living at 381 Bury Road, Breightmet, Bolton with his parents and brothers William b.1877, Tom b.1896 and Arthur b.1898.

In 1911 John was living at the same address with his parents and siblings William, Tom, Arthur, Gerald b.1902 and May b.1906.

John was employed as a railway clerk.

His name is on the Lancashire and Yorkshire Railway War Memorial on Victoria Station, Manchester.

Stanley Carter

Bolton Journal and Guardian 26 November 1915

Youthful Bolton Hero

Intimation has been received by his sister at 24, Eden-st., with whom he lived prior to enlisting, that **Pte. Stanley Carter** of the 11th Battalion Manchester Regiment, has been killed in the Dardanelles while landing. Though only 17* years of age he was of splendid physique. When he enlisted on January 16th he was employed on the farm of Mr. Jackson, Hall I'th' Wood, but prior to this he was a piecer at Messrs. Hesketh's Mills. He is an old scholar at Chalfont-st. Day School, and his name is on the roll of honour there.

Stanley was the son of Thomas Carter b.1870, a crofter in a bleachworks, and Alice Carter née Occleston b.1875.

Stanley appeared on the 1901 Census living at Flixton Road, Flixton with his parents and sisters Eva Occleston b.1896 and Gladys b.1900.

By 1911 Stanley's mother had died and the family had moved to 30 Clifford Street, Bolton.

Stanley was listed as working as a crofter like his father.

* Age wrongly given as 20 on CWGC records.

Name	Carter, Stanley
Rank	Private
Number	16672
Unit	11th Bn Manchester Regiment
Born	Flixton, Lancashire 1898
Enlisted	Manchester
Died	Malta 23 October 1915
Age	17
Grave or Memorial	Pieta Military Cemetery, Malta

Name	
Casement, Charles Edward	
Rank	
Private	
Number	
9457	
Unit	
1st Bn Border Regiment	
Born	
Bolton, Lancashire 1893	
Enlisted	
Bury, Lancashire	
Died	
Gallipoli, Turkey 23 August 1915	
Age	
22	
Grave or Memorial	
Helles Memorial, Gallipoli, Turkey	

Charles Edward Casement

Bolton Journal and Guardian 10 September 1915

Borderer Dies from Wounds

Following upon the announcement that **Private Chas. E. Casement** (9457), 1st Border Regiment, had been wounded in the fighting in Gallipoli, comes the sad news that he has succumbed to his injuries. Private Casement was 22 years of age. His parents reside at 65 Crumpsall-st., Bolton. He enlisted in the Border Regiment when 14 years of age, joining the band. He spent five years in India, and returned to England in February this year. After a few days' leave they were sent to the Dardanelles, where he took part in the historic landing, and was wounded in the left fore-arm on the second day, April 27th. He came over to England where he was a patient at the Flixton Hospital. When his wounds were healed he went to the Border Regiment depot at Shoeburyness, afterwards proceeding to join his regiment in Gallipoli. He was wounded, this time on August 21st, and death took place two days later. His brother, James Arthur, is in the 3/5th Loyal North Lancashire Regiment at Weeton, whilst his father was for some years bandmaster of the Loyal North Lancashire Regiment.

Charles was the son of John Casement b.1856, a school attendance officer, and Matilda Kate Casement née Rose b.1863.

He appeared on the 1901 Census living at 59 Davenport Street, Bolton with his parents and siblings Margaret Matilda b.1885, Elizabeth Sarah b.1886, Gertrude Louisa b.1888, Hilda Frances b.1889 and James Arthur b.1896.

By 1911 Charles was serving in the Army while his parents, along with Gertrude Louisa and James Arthur were living at 7 Norton Street, Bolton.

Percy Chapman

Percy was the son of Aaron Chapman b.1835, a coal miner, and Elizabeth Chapman née Bingham b.1837.

Percy first appeared on the 1881 Census living at Market Street, Clay Cross Derbyshire with his parents and siblings, Albert Henry b.1859, William b.1861, Edwin James b.1864, Clara b.1866, Emily b.1870, Florry b.1873, Elizabeth b.1875 and Ernest b.1877.

In 1891 he was living at 26 Bent Street, Kearsley with his parents and siblings Clara, Emily, Elizabeth, Ernest and Everard b.1882.

Percy was living at 36 Bent Street, Farnworth when he enlisted in the Lancashire Fusiliers at Bury in August 1897. He had previously been in the Militia as part of of 2nd Volunteer Bn Loyal North Lancashire Regiment.

On his medical examination he was recorded as being 5' 8 3/8" tall, weighing 125 lbs with a sallow complexion, dark grey eyes and brown hair. He had a tattoo of a line and a dot on his left forearm.

His previous occupation was given as collier.

He transferred as a regular soldier to 1st Bn Border Regiment on 1 September 1897.

He appeared on the 1911 Census as a private soldier with 1st Bn Border Regiment stationed in Burma.

He received a shrapnel wound in the back.

His name is on Kearsley War Memorial.

Name	
	Chapman, Percy
Rank	
	Private
Number	
	5528
Unit	
	1st Bn Border Regiment
Born	
	Clay Cross, Derbyshire 1879
Enlisted	
	Bury, Lancashire
Died	
	Netley Hospital, Hampshire 11 August 1916
Age	
	36
Grave or Memorial	
	Farnworth Cemetery, Farnworth, Lancashire

George Edwin Clark

Bolton Journal and Guardian 3 September 1915

Bolton Scout-master Killed

Writing to the "Journal and Guardian" from Gallipoli, Sergt. J. Horner, of the 6th East Lancashire Brigade, and formerly of 2, Melville-st., Great Lever, says:- "Will you kindly publish in your valuable paper the news of the death of **Sergt. Geo. E. Clark**, 6th East Lancashire Regiment, British Mediterranean Expeditionary Force, who was killed in action on August 9th. He was late Scoutmaster of some troop of Scouts in Bolton, and as a Bolton man myself, I thought it would be best to have it published in your paper, not knowing his wife's address. We were making a bayonet charge about 4.30 a. m. on the 8th, when Clark was shot through the head, death being instantaneous. As I was only a couple of yards from him when this occurred, I can assure his wife that he died game with his face to the enemy. We buried him at night as throughout that day the Turks were using machine guns all around where he fell. Hoping this will meet the eye of his wife, who has the sympathy of all the sergeants of the regiment. I will close, wishing your paper the best of luck."

Sergt George Edwin Clark, who lived at 14, Bristol-avenue, Tonge Moor, was formerly a machine man with Mr. J. W. Gledsdale printer, Deansgate, and was a member of the Bolton branch of the Typographical Association. He took a great interest in the Boy Scout movement, and was for some years secretary of the Bolton Scouts Association. He was Scoutmaster of the Bolton 3rd Troop. Most of his boys were connected with the Queen-st. Mission School, and he was a regular attender there up to the time of his enlistment last November. He joined the 6th East Lancashire Regiment, and went out to Gallipoli in June. He came to Bolton from Liverpool nine years ago. He had been brought up in that city from being a boy. He was exceedingly well-known in Bolton, however, and much sympathy will be extended to his wife and two children. Sergt Clark was 35 years of age.

George married Lily Trousdale b.1885, in Liverpool in 1906.

They had two children, Violet Brenda Clark b.1908 and Lilian B Clark b.1912.

They appeared on the 1911 Census living at 14 Bristol Avenue, Tonge Moor, Bolton.

George was employed as a printing machine minder.

Name
Clark, George Edwin
Rank
Sergeant
Number
17639
Unit
6th Bn East Lancashire Regiment
Born
Retford, Nottinghamshire 1879
Enlisted
November 1914
Died
Gallipoli, Turkey 9 August 1915
Age
35
Grave or Memorial
Helles Memorial, Gallipoli, Turkey

Joseph Collier

Bolton Journal and Guardian 14 January 1916

A Dardanelles Hero

Private Joseph Collier, 13th Lancashire Fusiliers, was killed in action in the Dardanelles on December 16th last. He was the only support of his aged parents, with whom he resided at 29, Pickering-st., Deane-rd. He was a single man, and previous to enlistment, 14 months ago, he was a side piecer at the Melrose Spinning Company's Mill. He would have been 36 years old tomorrow.

Joseph was the son of William Collier b.1846, a cotton overlooker, and Elizabeth Collier née Gaw b.1847.

In 1911 he was living at 1 Pocket, Blackshaw Lane, Bolton with his parents and his sister Betsy b.1873, who was listed as head of household. Betsy's son, Stanley b.1906 was also living there.

Joseph's occupation was given as cooper at that point but he was unemployed.

The 1911 Census also recorded that William and Elizabeth had had a total of 22 children of whom 15 had died and 7 survived.

Name	
Collier, Joseph	
Rank	
Private	
Number	
9662	
Unit	
1st Bn Lancashire Fusiliers	
Born	
Bolton, Lancashire 1879	
Enlisted	
Bury, Lancashire 1914	
Died	
Gallipoli, Turkey 16 December 1915	
Age	
35	
Grave or Memorial	
Lancashire Landing Cemetery, Gallipoli, Turkey	

Reuben Coop

Bolton Journal and Guardian 13 October 1916

Colonial Missing at the Dardanelles

The news that his son, **Pte. R. Coop**, No. 349 C Company, 9th Battalion 3rd Brigade, 1st Division Australian imperial Force, is missing has been received from the War Office by Mr. G. Coop, 231, Willows Lane, Bolton. The gallant young colonial was in action at the Dardanelles about the end of June, and since then nothing has been heard of him. A joiner by trade, he emigrated to Australia about nine years ago and was employed in Brisbane.

AIF Witness statement: Pte W. A. Page, 1865 B Co, 9 A.I.F. O/S base, Giza, Cairo

Coop was shot by the side of witness on June 28, on the left near Tasman Post, Just in front of Gun Ridge. He was cut almost in halves by machine gun fire, and died immediately. This happened during a demonstration made to draw the Turkish fire, during which 178 out of 250 men were knocked out. A party went out to bring the bodies in, but had to give up as machine guns were turned on them. Coop's body was, therefore, not recovered.

9th Battalion Unit Diary - 28 June 1915

Two companies (B and C Companies) provided to attack Sniper's Ridge south and Razor Back Ridge. C Company moved out of the 12th Btn trenches and B Company debouched from the dump in front of 11th Btn. Major Walsh commanded B Company and Captain Young, C Company. The attack was made with the object of co-operating with the Southern force and preventing the enemy from sending re-inforcements down. The attack of B Company was well carried out. C Company was under heavy fire from both flanks both shrapnel and machine guns, this attack was not well carried out and a retirement took place without orders from the company commander. The attack commenced at 1pm and B Company was ordered to retire at 2:50pm. The casualties were heavy. The missing in B Company are almost certain to be killed. It is possible that of the 15 missing in C Company the party under Lieut. Jordan may be prisoners.

Reuben was the son of George Coop b.1842, a grocer/provision dealer, and Betsy Coop née Entwistle b.1843

George and Betsy's children were listed on the 1871 Census as Simeon b.1867 and Reuben b.1870.

By 1891 the first Reuben had died and Simeon had been joined by Charles b.1874, George b.1879 and Margaret Hannah b.1881.

The second Reuben first appeared on the 1891 Census.

By 1901 the family were living at 344 Deane Road and Reuben was working as a joiner's apprentice.

Reuben's mother died in 1907.

Reuben set sail from Liverpool for Sydney, Australia aboard the SS Essex on 28 March 1908.

By the 1911 Census George Coop had retired and was living with his daughter (Margaret) Hannah who had married James Leach.

Name	
Coop, Reuben	
Rank	
Private	
Number	
349	
Unit	
9th Bn Australian Imperial Force	
Born	
Bolton, Lancashire 1885	
Enlisted	
Enoggera, Queensland, Australia 20 August 1914	
Died	
Gallipoli, Turkey 28 June 1915	
Age	
30	
Grave or Memorial	
Lone Pine Memorial, Gallipoli, Turkey	

Mark Coups

Bolton Journal and Guardian 24 December 1915

Two Horwich Soldiers Killed

Mr. and Mrs. Christopher Coupes (sic), 17 Smeaton-st., Horwich, have received an intimation from the War Office that their son, **Private Mark Coupes** (11842), of the 6th Battalion, L.N.L. Regiment was killed in the Dardanelles on August 10th. Pte. Coupes was 20 years of age and enlisted on the 24th of August last year. After having been in training at Salisbury, Winchester and Aldershot, he went to the Dardanelles in June last. Deceased was employed as an engine cleaner at the Loco. Works prior to enlisting. He was also a fairly well-known footballer and billiard player. In connexion with his football capabilities he recently won a medal given by the officers of his company. He was well-known in Horwich, and joined the army at the same time in the Dardanelles on August 10th. Pte. Coupes was 20 years of age, and enlisted on the 24th of August last as another soldier, who has given his life for his country, Pte. Richard Tickle, whose regimental number was 11841, whilst Pte. Coupes was 11842.

Mark was the son of Christopher Dransfield Coups b.1868, a railway clerk, and Julietta Martin Coups née Tress b.1870.

In 1911 the family lived in Smeaton Street, Horwich and consisted of Mark, his parents and siblings Christopher b.1898, May Eliza b.1901, Thomas b.1903, James b.1907 and Frank b.1910.

Mark's name is on the Horwich Loco Works War Memorial.

Name	
	Coups, Mark
Rank	
	Private
Number	
	11842
Unit	
	6th Bn
	The Loyal North
	Lancashire Regiment
Born	
	Manchester
	1895
Enlisted	
	Horwich, Lancashire
	24 August 1914
Died	
	Gallipoli, Turkey
	10 August 1915
Age	
	20
Grave or Memorial	
	Helles Memorial,
	Gallipoli, Turkey

Albert Robert Dawson

Bolton Journal and Guardian 5 November 1915

Fought at Gaba Tepe

The death of another Boltonian with the Australian contingent in the person of **Bugler Albert Robert Dawson** is announced. Prior to going to Victoria three years ago Dawson, whose relatives live in the Daubhill district, was employed as an iron turner at Dobson and Barlow's. Dawson, who was one of the first volunteers to leave for the front in October, was in the ill-fated 3rd Battalion and went through the landing at Gaba Tepe unscathed. He was 25 years of age, and leaves a young widow and three children.

Cumberland Argus and Fruitgrowers' Advocate 11 September 1915

Bugler Albert Robert Dawson - Killed in action

He was amongst the first of our volunteers to leave for the front, in October last, and was attached to the ill-fated 3rd Battalion. He was with the landing party at Gaba Tepe, and went through the trying ordeal unscathed. He was 25 years of age and leaves a widow and three little children, not too well provided for. They reside in a small semi-detached cottage in Woodburn-road, Lidcombe. The subject of our notice had only been out here three years from England. His mother resides at Waverley: he has a younger brother at the front, and another only 18 years of age now in camp. His wife received word officially of his death on the 2nd inst. He was killed in action on 4th of August. On the 8th inst. she received from him a few lines written on a piece of cardboard dated 29th July, from the trenches in Gallipoli. He stated: "I am in good health. There is nothing doing, only plenty of work. The enemy has been sticking plenty of shell into our trenches lately, but without doing much damage." Previous to that a rather lengthy letter was received by Mrs. Dawson, dated 12th July. In it he said: "It is fairly quiet at present as far as fighting is concerned. The warships are bombarding the enemy on our right flank, and our artillery and the enemy are having a bit of a go at each other. Of course, this is an every day occurrence. We keep up a bit of sniping at the enemy's trenches, which are only 90 yards in front of us, and they do the same to us and try to get at one another's loop holes. It is quite a long time since we saw a Turk. We never see anything now, only a bit of dust or a rifle flash to fire at. Of course you can bet we don't show much of ourselves over the parapet. You should see the flies over here. They are ready to eat one. There are millions of them at meal times. They nearly drink the tea on us. I am receiving instructions on a machine gun. I expect to be in that section shortly.

Albert was the son of Robert Dawson b.1866, a safe maker, and Mary Ellen Dawson née Wash B.1870

On the 1891 Census he was living at 4 Lomax Buildings, Bradshawgate, Bolton with his parents.

Albert married Annie Roylance in Bolton in 1910. The couple appeared on the 1911 Census living at at 14 Albert Street, Bolton with thier daughter Ivy b.1911. His occupation was given as iron roller spacer. A son, Albert was born late in 1911.

The family sailed for Sydney, Australia in August 1912 where Albert intended to start a new life as a farmer.

His medical report on enlistment recorded him as being 5' 7" tall and weighing 10st 2lb with fair complexion, brown eyes and fair curly hair. He had a tattoo of Prince of Wales feathers and a star on his right forearm.

Name	
Dawson, Albert Robert	
Rank	
Buglar	
Number	
1091	
Unit	
3rd Bn Australian Imperial Force	
Born	
Bolton, Lancashire 1889	
Enlisted	
Randwick, Sydney, NSW, Australia 17 August 1914	
Died	
Gallipoli, Turkey 4 August 1915	
Age	
25	
Grave or Memorial	
Shrapnel Valley Cemetery, Gallipoli, Turkey	

John Dearden

Bolton Journal and Guardian 24 December 1915

Yeomanry Sergeant Killed

The Bolton Troop of the Duke of Lancaster's Own Yeomanry has lost one of its best known and most popular members by the death of **Sergt. John Dearden**, of 31, Avenue-st. which took place on the Gallipoli Peninsula in November, as the result of wounds. Sergt. Dearden has been engaged on Military Mounted Police work on the Peninsula for the last eight months, and a letter from a colleague, Corporal G. Taylor, states that the two were on patrol duty along with others when a shell burst near them and a flying splinter struck Dearden on the head. He was removed to hospital and an operation successfully performed, but later he had a relapse and died. Sergt. Dearden, who was 32 years of age, and is an old boy of St. Matthew's School has always been interested in military life, and at the age of 14 he joined the Boys' Brigade. Two years later he went to South Africa as Trumpeter to the Bolton Volunteers, and served with them through the Boer War, and on his return he joined the Yeomanry in the same capacity, afterwards serving as a trooper and being promoted sergeant. He was exceedingly popular with the troop, and acted as treasurer. About 18 months ago, when General Methuen visited Bolton, he had the honour of leading the procession. In private life he was a spinner, having been employed by Haslam Spinning Company Ltd., for the last 22 years, or since he was 10 years of age. Great sympathy will be extended to Mrs. Dearden and her five children, the eldest of whom is only 11 years of age.

John was the son of Peter Dearden b.1858, a cotton bleacher, and Margaret Dearden b.1856.

On the 1891 Census he was living at 89 Mount Street with his parents and siblings William b.1885, Annie b.1887 and Margaret b.1890.

By 1901 the family were living at 19 Avenue Street, Bolton with the the addition of children Emily b.1893 and James b.1898. John was not present.

John married Betsy Wood b.1882 in 1902. He was then working as a self actor minder in a textile mill.

They appear on the 1911 Census living at 104 John Brown Street, Bolton with children Edna b.1904 John b.1906 Robert b.1908 and William b.1909.

Another son, Reginald, was born in 1915.

Name	Dearden, John
Rank	Sergeant
Number	1924
Unit	1/1st Bn Duke of Lancaster's Own Yeomanry
Born	Bolton, Lancashire c.1883
Enlisted	Bolton
Died	Gallipoli, Turkey 25 November 1915
Age	32
Grave or Memorial	Lancashire Landing Cemetery, Gallipoli, Turkey

James Edmund Denton

Bolton Journal and Guardian 10 September 1915

MISSING IN GALLIPOLI

In an engagement on the Gallipoli Peninsula on August 9th, the 6th Battalion Loyal North Lancashire Regiment, seems to have suffered heavily, a number of casualties to Bolton soldiers in that unit having been reported...

An official notice has also been received by the wife of **Pte. James Denton** (11335), 6th Battalion L.N.L. Regiment, 81, Morris Green-lane, informing her that he has been missing since the same engagement. He enlisted on June 17th, 1914, and prior to that was engaged as a guard on the L. and N.W. Railway. He attended Foundry-st. Mission.

James was the son of Joseph Denton and Edna Denton née Howarth.

He first appeared on the 1891 Census living at 20 Kirk Street, Bolton with his grandparents, Edmund and Betsy Howarth and their children.

In 1901 he was living at 40 Kirk Street with his widowed grandmother and family.

He was working then as an apprentice machine fitter.

James married Annie Lord at St Mary the Virgin Church, Deane, Bolton in 1905.

Name	Denton, James Edmund
Rank	Private
Number	11335
Unit	6th Bn The Loyal North Lancashire Regiment
Born	Bolton, Lancashire 1885
Enlisted	Bolton, Lancashire 17 June 1914
Died	Gallipoli, Turkey 9 August 1915
Age	29
Grave or Memorial	Helles Memorial, Gallipoli, Turkey

Robert Derbyshire

Bolton Journal and Guardian 18 June 1915

Died from Wounds

News is to hand that **Pte. Robert Darbyshire** (sic), R.M.L.I. had died in Hospital at Alexandria as the result of wounds received in the Dardanelles. He resided at 32, Grecian-st., Great Lever. He was 19 years of age and enlisted in September. As a boy he attended St. George the Martyr's School, and was a member of the Mawdsley-st. P.S.A.* He was employed before the outbreak of war as a piecer at Robin Hood Mills, Lever-st.

Robert was the son of Thomas Derbyshire b.1868, an operative cotton spinner, and Louisa Gertrude Derbyshire née Walker b.1868.

Robert appeared on the 1901 Census living with his parents at 1 Dijon Street, Bolton.

By 1911 he was living at 19 Essingdon Street with his parents and brother James b.1904.

At the age of 13 Robert was working as a cotton mule piecer.

Robert died of wounds in No.11 Casualty Clearing Station 'W' Beach (Gun shot wound to head).

* *PSA = Pleasant Sunday Afternoon*

**CWGC has him buried in Gallipoli but the article suggests he died in Egypt.*

Name
Derbyshire, Robert
Rank
Private
Number
PLY/357(S)
Unit
Plymouth Bn Royal Naval Division, Royal Marine Light Infantry
Born
Bolton, Lancashire 1897
Enlisted
September 1914
Died
Gallipoli, Turkey** 29 May 1915
Age
19
Grave or Memorial
Lancashire Landing Cemetery, Gallipoli, Turkey

Name
Dolan, James
Rank
Private
Number
11605
Unit
6th Bn
The Loyal North
Lancashire Regiment
Born
Farnworth, Lancashire
1886
Enlisted
Preston, Lancashire
September 1914
Died
Gallipoli, Turkey
10 August 1915
Age
29
Grave or Memorial
Helles Memorial,
Gallipoli, Turkey

James Dolan

Farnworth Weekly Journal 17 September 1915

KILLED IN ACTION

Mr. R. H. Dolan (sic) of 29, Bentinck-st, Farnworth, has received word that his son, **Pte. James Dolan** (11605), aged 29 of the 6th L.N.L., was killed in action at the Dardanelles on August 10th. Previous to joining the Army in September last year Pte. Dolan was a shoemaker, working at Stockport. He left for the Dardanelles in June. According to his last letter he reached the firing line about July 6th. In a letter of that date he stated:-"I am going into the firing line tonight to do my little bit. I cannot say much about this place except that the weather is terribly dry." Pte. J. Dolan's brother, Pte. ? Dolan of 2 Green-st, Bolton, is in the L/N.L. and has been in France for nine months, and his step-brother, Pte. J. W. Flitcroft (5386), is also in the Army and training in the 4/5th L.N.L., which he joined three months ago.

James was the son of Richard Armistead Dolan b.1855, a labourer and previously a coal miner, and Sarah Ellen Dolan née Grimshaw b.1857.

James first appeared on the 1891 Census when he was lodging at 20 Kent Street, Farnworth with his father and siblings Margaret S b.1877 and Richard b.1884.

In 1901 - aged 14 - James was a pupil/inmate of Bishop Brown Memorial Industrial School for Roman Catholic Boys, Stockport.

His employment was given as shoemaker.

In 1901 his father was lodging at 4 Rose Street, Farnworth.

James's father, Richard, remarried to Mary Jane Flitcroft on 22 November 1902.

In 1911 James was living in a lodging house at 76 Dock Street, Fleetwood, Lancashire.

He was still working as a shoemaker.

James's name is on Farnworth War Memorial.

James Doyle

Farnworth War Memorial was unveiled by **James Stones**, Chairman of Farnworth UDC in November 1924. His son **John Stones** is on the memorial, having been killed in action in France in April 1918.

The Memorial was re-dedicated by HRH The Duke of Gloucester on 27 April 2005.

James Drury

James's name appears on the Bolton Borough Roll of Honour.

Name	*Drury, James*
Rank	*Private*
Number	*8814*
Unit	*1st Bn Border Regiment*
Born	
Enlisted	
Died	*Gallipoli, Turkey* *23 August 1915*
Age	
Grave or Memorial	*Helles Memorial, Gallipoli, Turkey*

Robert Durning

Bolton Journal and Guardian 17 September 1915

Private Robert Durning (12534), attached to C Company of the 6th Loyal North Lancashire Regiment, has also been posted as missing from August 9th. He is a well-built young fellow of 23, and has been serving the colours since August, 1914. On enlisting he was drafted to Preston for training, later to Tidworth, Winchester, and Blackdown, leaving for the Dardanelles in June. He was formerly employed at Messrs. Tootal Broadhurst Lee Company's Mill, Daubhill, and resided with his parents at 18, Grendon-st, Morris Green-lane.

Bolton Journal and Guardian 22 September 1916

His parents chief support, **Pte. ROBT. DURNING**, Loyal North Lancashire Regiment, has just been reported killed in the Gallipoli campaign on August 9th, 1915, since which date nothing has been heard of him. He was an old Sunning Hill schoolboy, residing at 18, Grendon-st., Bolton, and worked as a beam carrier at the Tootal Broadhurst Lee Company's mill. Durning's name is on the Roll of Honour at Morris Green Church.

Robert was the son of Robert Durning b.1857, an engine driver, and Margaret Durning née Grice b.1851.

Margaret had children from a previous relationship: Mary Grice b.1876 and John Robert Grice b.1879.

The Grice children appeared as Durnings on the 1891 Census when the family were living in Sutton, St Helens, Lancashire. There were four other daughters: Ellen b.1882, Margaret b.1884, Martha Jubilee b.1887 and Sarah b.1890.

Robert's father died in 1896 and by 1901 the family were living at 24 Sunninghill Street, Bolton.

In 1911 they were living at 18 Grendon Street, Morris Green, Bolton.

Robert was working as a piecer.

Robert's medical examination on enlisting in the Army recorded him as being 5' 7 1/4" tall, weighing 128 lbs with a fresh complexion, blue eyes and brown hair.

Name	Durning, Robert
Rank	Private
Number	12534
Unit	6th Bn The Loyal North Lancashire Regiment
Born	Sutton, St Helens, Lancashire 1892
Enlisted	Bolton, Lancashire 29 August 1914
Died	Gallipoli, Turkey 9 August 1915
Age	23
Grave or Memorial	Helles Memorial, Gallipoli, Turkey

Norman Edwardson

Bolton Journal and Guardian 12 November 1915

Daisy Hill Goalkeeper Dies at Malta

Mr. Thomas Edwardson, 8, St. James-st., Daisy Hill, has received official information that his son, **Pte. Norman Edwardson** (20173), 1st Border Regiment, has died of dysentery in the hospital at Malta. The deceased soldier enlisted at Atherton in April, this year in the 3rd Border Regiment. He did his training at Shoeburyness and was afterwards transferred to the 1st Border Regiment, and sailed for the Dardanelles at the end of August. He was 17 years of age, was employed at Messrs. Fletcher, Burrows and Company's Arley mine, and attended Daisy Hill St. James's Church and Sunday School. He was also goalkeeper for Daisy Hill second team in the Leigh and District Sunday School League. Another brother (Ernest) who was a player with the second team of Daisy Hill Cricket Club, has enlisted in the King's Own Royal Lancasters and been in France since April.

Norman was the son of Thomas Edwardson b.1859, a builder's labourer who had previously worked as a coal miner and in cotton mills, and Ann Edwardson née Halliday b.1858.

On the 1881 Census Thomas and Ann were living in Wigan and had two sons, John b.1879 and James b.1880.

By 1891 the family had moved to 34 New Sirs, Westhoughton. James was no longer with them but there are four new children: Mary Jane b.1882, Edith b.1885, Rachel b.1887 and Thomas b.1891.

On the 1901 Census the family were living at 1 Old Sirs, Westhoughton and had been joined by Norman, Ernest b.1894 and Ethel b.1896.

In 1911 the family were still at the same address and Norman was working as a labourer in a print works.

His medical examination on enlisting in the Army records him as being 5' 6 1/2" tall and 143 lbs.

His name is on Westhoughton War Memorial.

Name	Ratcliffe, James
Rank	Private
Number	20173
Unit	1st Bn Border Regiment
Born	Westhoughton, Lancashire 1898
Enlisted	Atherton, Lancashire 8 April 1915
Died	Gallipoli, Turkey 6 October 1915
Age	17
Grave or Memorial	Hill 10 Cemetery, Gallipoli, Turkey

Name
Edge, Thomas
Rank
Private
Number
2198
Unit
1st Bn Lancashire Fusiliers
Born
Bolton, Lancashire 1888
Enlisted
Bury, Lancashire
Died
Gallipoli, Turkey 28 April 1915
Age
27
Grave or Memorial
Helles Memorial Gallipoli, Turkey

Thomas Edge

Thomas was the son of Thomas Edge b.1848, a fish hawker, and Jane Ann Edge née Conway b.1857.

Jane Ann had previously been married to John Flitcroft.

Thomas first appeared on the 1891 Census living at 6 Spring Street, Bolton with his parents, sister Bertha b.1890 and step-sisters Martha Ann Flitcroft b.1880, Elizabeth Flitcroft b.1884 and Margaret A Flitcroft b.1885.

In 1901 he was living at 2 Thompson Square, Bolton with his parents and step-sisters Elizabeth and Margaret A Flitcroft. At 13 he was already working as a piecer in a cotton mill.

He briefly joined the Militia as a private in the Lancashire Fusiliers at Bury in March 1905. He was passed as fit at his medical but was discharged as "permanently unfit for further service" a few weeks later.

In July 1906 he joined the Manchester Regiment at Ashton-under-Lyne. His medical examination recorded him as being 5' 7" tall, weighing 111 lbs and having a fresh complexion, brown eyes and dark brown hair.

He transferred to the Royal Field Artillery in January 1907.

He was caught receiving stolen goods and discharged from the Army in September 1908 after being 'convicted by the Civil Power' and given 6 months hard labour.

A Thomas Edge, born in Bolton, appeared as a private soldier with the Lancashire Fusiliers at their barracks in South Tidworth, Hampshire on the 1911 Census, although listed as being born c.1892.

Robert Evans

Robert's name appears on the Bolton Borough Roll of Honour.

Name	
Evans, Robert	
Rank	
Lance Corporal	
Number	
19128	
Unit	
1st Bn	
Border Regiment	
Born	
Enlisted	
Died	
Gallipoli, Turkey	
28 April 1915	
Age	
Grave or Memorial	
Helles Memorial,	
Gallipoli, Turkey	

Harold Fairhurst

Bolton Journal and Guardian

Fate of Astley Bridge Soldier

Another member of the 6th Battalion, L.N.L. Regiment, **Pte.** (14,998) **Harold Fairhurst** has been reported missing after an engagement on August 9th. Pte. Fairhurst was 19 years of age, and before enlisting was employed in the warehouse of No. 2 North End Spinning Co. He was well known in the Astley Bridge district, where he resided with his parents at 53, Cameron-st. He enlisted on Nov. 10th, last year, and after training at Preston, Tidworth, Winchester and Blackdown, went to the Dardanelles about the middle of June.

Harold was the son of Matthew Fairhurst b.1873, an insurance agent with the Refuge Assurance Society and sometime cotton finisher, and Mary Jane Fairhurst née Austin b.1872.

He appeared on the 1901 Census living with his parents, his mother's sister, Susannah Austin and her brother Mark Austin at 45 Cameron Street, Bolton.

By 1911 the family had moved to 53 Cameron Street, Mark Austin was no longer living with them but Harold was working as a warehouse boy in a cotton mill and had a new brother, Herbert Austin Fairhurst b.1907.

Harold's medical examination on enlisting in the Army recorded him as being 5' 4" tall, 112 lbs with a fresh complexion, grey eyes and brown hair.

His occupation was given as labourer.

Name	Fairhurst, Harold
Rank	Private
Number	14998
Unit	6th Bn The Loyal North Lancashire Regiment
Born	Bolton, Lancashire 1896
Enlisted	Bolton, Lancashire 1914
Died	Gallipoli, Turkey 9 August 1915
Age	19
Grave or Memorial	Helles Memorial, Gallipoli, Turkey

Joseph Farnworth

Bolton Journal and Guardian 18 August 1916

Pte. Joseph Farnworth, Border Regiment, is a victim of the Dardanelles campaign. On August 21st, 1915, he was observed to be dressing the wounds of a comrade whilst under fire, but nothing has been seen or heard of him since, and his parents have been informed by the War Office that they are now constrained to believe that he is dead. Deceased, who was a dental mechanic* for Mr. Clegg, of Hindley, was a member of a family now resident in Ordsall-lane, Salford, but formerly of Auburn-st, Daubhill. Deceased, who was 28 and unmarried, enlisted soon after the outbreak of war.

Joseph was the son of James Farnworth b.1861, an engineer / mechanic in a cotton mill, and Jane Farnworth née Healey b.1863

Joseph first appeared on the 1891 Census living at 24 Auburn Street with his parents and brother Albert b.1889.

In 1901 the family were living at 5 Cecil Street, Ordsall, Salford, Lancashire.

By 1911 they were all living at 390 Ordsall Lane, Salford.

Joseph was then employed as an iron fitter in a cotton mill.

* *His maternal grandfather had been a dentist.*

Name	Farnworth, Joseph
Rank	Private
Number	19128
Unit	1st Bn Border Regiment
Born	Bolton, Lancashire c.1887
Enlisted	Bolton, Lancashire January 1915
Died	Gallipoli, Turkey 21 August 1915
Age	27
Grave or Memorial	Helles Memorial, Gallipoli, Turkey

John Fielding

Bolton Journal and Guardian 21 May 1915

Local Soldiers Killed in the Dardanelles

News is to hand that Mrs. Fielding, Tonge Green Farm, Tonge Moor, has received official information that her son, **Private J. Fielding**, was killed in action on May 11th in the Dardanelles. He was attached to the Lancashire Fusiliers, and enlisted seven months ago, four of which have been spent in India. He enjoyed a brief furlough in January.

Note difference in official death date on CWGC.

Name	Fielding, John
Rank	Private
Number	1808
Unit	1st Bn Lancashire Fusiliers
Born	Bolton, Lancashire
Enlisted	Bolton, Lancashire 1914
Died	Gallipoli, Turkey 25 April 1915
Age	
Grave or Memorial	Helles Memorial, Gallipoli, Turkey

Albert Fisher

Bolton Journal and Guardian 3 September 1915

Four Brothers. Three Killed in One Battle

Of the Four'sons of Mr. and Mrs. Wm. (sic) Fisher, 280, Deane Church-lane, Bolton, who have joined the forces, three have been killed and one has been wounded. The latter is Pte. Harry, of the 1/5th Battalion L.N.I., and he is the youngest of the quartet. He has been injured by shrapnel in the left ankle. He was an enthusiastic footballer, and played with one of the tradesmen's clubs in the Bolton Wednesday League. The three who have been killed, Privates **Albert**, Matthew and Jack, were all members of the 6th L.N.L., and fell during two days hard fighting in the Dardanelles. Before the war all three were engaged as minders in Bolton Mills. **Albert**, who was the oldest, leaves a wife, Matthew a wife and four children, and Jack a wife and two children. All were well known in Deane, though Albert had latterly lived in St Anne-st., Halliwell-rd., and Matthew in Tonge Moor. Jack was a great swimmer, and recovered two of the three bodies of the Westhoughton children who were drowned at Rumworth over 12 months ago. He also recovered a little girl from a lodge close to his home. All the brothers enlisted when the war broke out, though Matthew had been in the Army previously, and taken part in the Boer War. Jack was formerly in the Bolton Military Band.

Albert was the son of John Fisher b.1859, a cotton spinner, and Mary Fisher b.1858.

Albert married Anne Ellen Brough b.1882 at St Matthew's Church, Bolton in 1904.

He was living with his wife at 37 Argyle Street in 1911. They had had two children but both had died.

Name	Fisher, Albert
Rank	Private
Number	17425
Unit	6th Bn The Loyal North Lancashire Regiment
Born	Bolton, Lancashire c.1882
Enlisted	Bolton, Lancashire
Died	Gallipoli, Turkey 9 August 1915
Age	33
Grave or Memorial	Helles Memorial, Gallipoli, Turkey

John Fisher

Bolton Journal and Guardian 3 September 1915

Four Brothers. Three Killed in One Battle

Of the Four sons of Mr. and Mrs. Wm. (sic) Fisher, 280, Deane Church-lane, Bolton, who have joined the forces, three have been killed and one has been wounded. The latter is Pte. Harry, of the 1/5th Battalion L.N.I., and he is the youngest of the quartet. He has been injured by shrapnel in the left ankle. He was an enthusiastic footballer, and played with one of the tradesmen's clubs in the Bolton Wednesday League. The three who have been killed, Privates Albert, Matthew and **Jack**, were all members of the 6th L.N.L., and fell during two days hard fighting in the Dardanelles. Before the war all three were engaged as minders in Bolton Mills. Albert, who was the oldest, leaves a wife, Matthew a wife and four children, and Jack a wife and two children. All were well known in Deane, though Albert had latterly lived in St Anne-st., Halliwell-rd., and Matthew in Tonge Moor. **Jack** was a great swimmer, and recovered two of the three bodies of the Westhoughton children who were drowned at Rumworth over 12 months ago. He also recovered a little girl from a lodge close to his home. All the brothers enlisted when the war broke out, though Matthew had been in the Army previously, and taken part in the Boer War. Jack was formerly in the Bolton Military Band.

John (Jack) was the son of John Fisher b.1859, a cotton spinner, and Mary Fisher b.1858.

He married Sarah Ann Urmston b.1892 at Emmanuel Church, Bolton in 1910.

The family appeared on the 1911 Census living at 6 Back Harris Street, Bolton with their daughter, Emily b.1911.

He was working as a piecer in a cotton spinning mill.

Name	Fisher, John
Rank	Private
Number	12528
Unit	6th Bn The Loyal North Lancashire Regiment
Born	Bolton, Lancashire c.1887
Enlisted	Bolton, Lancashire
Died	Gallipoli, Turkey 10 August 1915
Age	28
Grave or Memorial	Helles Memorial, Gallipoli, Turkey

Joseph Fisher

Bolton Journal and Guardian 1915

Killed in the Dardanelles

Pte. Joseph Fisher (18676), 1st Batt. Border Regiment, has been killed in the Dardanelles. The deceased, who lived at 19, King-st., was an old militia man, and reported himself at the outbreak of the war. He had been at the Dardanelles since May 3rd, and was killed on August 21st. A native of Atherton, and a collier employed at Messrs. Scowcroft and Son's colliery, Long-lane, he was 28 years of age, and leaves a widow and one child. In his younger days he was well known as a wrestler and weight-lifter.

Bolton Journal and Guardian 1 October 1915

Killed in Gallipoli

The death is announced to have taken place in the Dardanelles, where he saw much fighting, of **Pte. Joseph Fisher** (18676), 1st Battalion Border Regiment. Deceased, who was 28 years of age, and leaves a widow and one child, was a native of Atherton, and prior to the call to arms at the commencement of hostilities was employed as a collier at Messrs. S. Scowcroft and Son's colliery, Long-lane. He was an old Militia man, and in his younger days was a well known wrestler and weight-lifter. In peace times he resided at 19, King-st.

Joseph was the son of John Fisher b.1857, a coal miner, and Ann Fisher b.1856.

Joseph first appeared on the 1891 Census living at 16 Spring Gardens, Atherton with his parents and siblings Mary (Margaret?) b.1876, John b.1878, William b.1879, Isaac b.1882, Tilda (?) b.1865 and Thomas b.1889.

In 1901 he was living at the same address with his parents and siblings Isaac, Thomas, Matilda b.1892, Edward, b.1894, Benjamin b.1896, Elizabeth b.1897 and Amelia b.1900.

Joseph was working at that point but his actual occupation is illegible on the census return.

In 1911 Joseph was living at 38 Spring Gardens, Bolton with Mary Ellen Gill b.1889 who was listed as a relative and her occupation as servant. She also filled in the Census form.

Joseph's place of birth was this time given as Millom, Cumberland.

His occupation then was collier/hewer in a coal mine.

Joseph married Mary Ellen Gill at St John the Baptist's Church, Atherton, Lancashire on 25 May 1912.

Name	
	Fisher, Joseph
Rank	
	Private
Number	
	18676
Unit	
	1st Bn Border Regiment
Born	
	Tipton, Staffordshire 1887
Enlisted	
	Bolton, Lancashire
Died	
	Gallipoli, Turkey 21 August 1915
Age	
	28
Grave or Memorial	
	Green Hill Cemetery, Gallipoli, Turkey

Name	
Fisher, Francis William	
Rank	
Private	
Number	
PLY/251(S)	
Unit	
Plymouth Bn Royal Naval Division, Royal Marine Light Infantry	
Born	
Farnworth, Lancashire 26 January 1896	
Enlisted	
1914	
Died	
Gallipoli, Turkey 4 September 1915	
Age	
19	
Grave or Memorial	
Helles Memorial, Gallipoli, Turkey	

Francis Wiliam Fisher

Farnworth Weekly Journal 1 October 1915

FARNWORTH GRAMMAR SCHOOL BOY KILLED

Mrs. Ellen Fisher, of Gladstone Villa, Gladstone-rd., Farnworth, has received official intimation from the Admiralty of the death in action on the Gallipoli Peninsula, on September 4th of her eldest son, **Pte. Francis W. Fisher** R.M.L.I., Plymouth battalion. Deceased was a Farnworth Grammar School old boy, and was 19 years of age. He worked for Messrs. H. H. Hutton, shippers, Manchester, enlisted on the outbreak of the war, and was with the first landing party at the Dardanelles. Three months ago he was wounded and was sent to hospital at Malta and after his recovery he rejoined his unit.

Francis was the son of James William Fisher b.1868, a ship broker, and Ellen Fisher née Challinor b.1865.

Francis appeared on the 1901 Census living at 1 Crosby Road South, Seaforth, Lancashire with his parents, brother Thomas Norman b.1899 and a female domestic servant.

His father died and in 1911 Francis was living at Gladstone Villa, Farnworth with his mother, brother and a female domestic servant.

Francis was educated at Farnworth Grammar School and was on the War Memorial there until the school was demolished after closing in 1982.

His name is also on Farnworth War Memorial.

Matthew Fisher

Bolton Journal and Guardian 3 September 1915

Four Brothers. Three Killed in One Battle

Of the Four sons of Mr. and Mrs. Wm. (sic) Fisher, 280, Deane Church-lane, Bolton, who have joined the forces, three have been killed and one has been wounded. The latter is Pte. Harry, of the 1/5th Battalion L.N.I., and he is the youngest of the quartet. He has been injured by shrapnel in the left ankle. He was an enthusiastic footballer, and played with one of the tradesmen's clubs in the Bolton Wednesday League. The three who have been killed, Privates Albert, **Matthew** and Jack, were all members of the 6th L.N.L., and fell during two days hard fighting in the Dardanelles. Before the war all three were engaged as minders in Bolton Mills. Albert, who was the oldest, leaves a wife, Matthew a wife and four children, and Jack a wife and two children. All were well known in Deane, though Albert had latterly lived in St Anne-st., Halliwell-rd., and **Matthew** in Tonge Moor. Jack was a great swimmer, and recovered two of the three bodies of the Westhoughton children who were drowned at Rumworth over 12 months ago. He also recovered a little girl from a lodge close to his home. All the brothers enlisted when the war broke out, though **Matthew** had been in the Army previously, and taken part in the Boer War. Jack was formerly in the Bolton Military Band.

Matthew was the son of John Fisher b.1859, a cotton spinner, and Mary Fisher b.1858.

Matthew married Alice b.1883 in 1904.

They were living at 4 Beta Street, Bolton in 1911 with their three children: Matthew b.1905, John b.1907 and William b.1910. They had also had another child who had died.

Matthew was working as a piecer in a cotton spinning mill in 1911.

Name
Fisher, Matthew
Rank
Private
Number
12517
Unit
6th Bn The Loyal North Lancashire Regiment
Born
Bolton, Lancashire c.1883
Enlisted
Bolton, Lancashire
Died
Gallipoli, Turkey 10 August 1915
Age
32
Grave or Memorial
Helles Memorial, Gallipoli, Turkey

Name
Fishwick, Thomas
Rank
Private
Number
17834
Unit
6th Bn
The Loyal North
Lancashire Regiment
Born
Farnworth, Lancashire
1897
Enlisted
Farnworth, Lancashire
1914
Died
Gallipoli, Turkey
9 August 1915
Age
18
Grave or Memorial
Helles Memorial,
Gallipoli, Turkey

Thomas Fishwick

Farnworth Weekly Journal 3 December 1915

NO NEWS YET

Mrs. Fishwick of 39, Victoria-st., Farnworth, has not yet received any word of her son **Pte. Thomas Fishwick**, aged 18 years, of the 6th Battalion L.N.L. (No. 17834), who was officially posted as missing on August 9th in the Dardanelles. Pte. Fishwick, who used to work at the Wet Earth Colliery of the Clifton and Kearsley Coal Company, enlisted a year ago, and went out to the Dardanelles in May. His last message home was a field service card dated July 31st., when he stated that he was all right. Prior to that he said he had just come out of the trenches, that the conditions were not bad,and that they had had very few casualties. Mrs. Fishwick would be pleased to hear from any soldier who has information about her son's whereabouts, or who saw him between July 31st and August 9th. Another of her sons is in the army - Driver Peter Fishwick, of the R.F.A., who enlisted in January from the Moses Gate goods yard.

Thomas was the son of Edward Fishwick b.1861, a self actor minder in a cotton mill, and Ellen Fishwick née Massey b.1863.

He first appeared on the 1901 living at 30 Lee Street, Farnworth with his parents and siblings Mary b.1887, John b.1890, Peter b.1894 and James b.1900.

By 1911 he was living at 39 Victoria Street, Moses Gate, Farnworth with his widowed mother and siblings John and Peter.

Thomas was working as a cotton mule piecer.

Thomas's name is on Farnworth War Memorial.

James Flanagan

Bolton Journal and Guardian 13 October 1915

Mother's Double Loss

Whilst entertaining fears for the safety of her son, James, who has been reported missing in Gallipoli, Mrs Flannagan (sic), 9, Royal-row, Crook-st., has now learned officially that another son, Lance-Corporal Thomas Flannagan, has died of dysentery. The brothers were both attached to the L.N.L. Regiment, and left for the Dardanelles about six weeks ago. Thomas, who was 28 years of age, leaves a wife and two children, who reside at 1 Whittaker-st. He was formerly employed by Messrs. Brown's waste merchants, Bridgeman-place. **Pte. James Flannagan** is 22 years of age, and prior to enlisting in October last year was a fitter at Messrs. Dobson and Barlow's, Bradley Fold. Both brothers worshipped at St. Patrick's.

James was the son of Patrick Flanagan b.1857 and Honora (Norah) Flanagan née Woods b.1861.

In 1901 James was living at 188 Blackhorse Street, Bolton with his parents and siblings Norah b.1881, Mary b.1883, Catherine (Katie) b.1885, Thomas b.1887, John b.1888 and Ellen b.1892.

The names of Thomas and his father Patrick appear to have been transposed by the ennumerator.

He appeared on the 1911 Census living with his widowed mother at 9 Royal Row, Bolton and his siblings, Mary b.1883, Catherine b.1885, John b.1888 and Ellen b.1892.

Name	Flanagan, James
Rank	Private
Number	17240
Unit	6th Bn The Loyal North Lancashire Regiment
Born	Bolton, Lancashire c.1893
Enlisted	Bolton, Lancashire
Died	Malta 9 August 1915
Age	22
Grave or Memorial	Helles Memorial, Gallipoli, Turkey

Thomas Flanagan

Bolton Journal and Guardian 13 October 1915

Mother's Double Loss

Whilst entertaining fears for the safety of her son, James, who has been reported missing in Gallipoli, Mrs Flannagan (sic), 9, Royal-row, Crook-st., has now learned officially that another son, Lance-**Corporal Thomas Flannagan**, has died of dysentery. The brothers were both attached to the L.N.L. Regiment, and left for the Dardanelles about six weeks ago. Thomas, who was 28 years of age, leaves a wife and two children, who reside at 1 Whittaker-st. He was formerly employed by Messrs. Brown's waste merchants, Bridgeman-place. Pte. James Flannagan is 22 years of age, and prior to enlisting in October last year was a fitter at Messrs. Dobson and Barlow's, Bradley Fold. Both brothers worshipped at St. Patrick's.

Thomas was the son of Patrick Flanagan b.1857 and Honora (Norah) Flanagan née Woods b.1861.

He appeared on the 1891 Census living at 2 Bolling Street, Bolton with his parents and siblings, Norah b.1881, Mary b.1883, Catherine b.1885 and John b.1888.

In 1901 Thomas was living at 188 Blackhorse Street, Bolton with his parents and siblings Norah b.1881, Mary, Catherine (Katie), John b.1888, Ellen b.1892 and James b.1893.

The names of Thomas and his father Patrick appear to have been transposed by the ennumerator.

Thomas married Phoebe Anne Leigh b.1887 in Bolton in 1910.

On the 1911 Census they were living at 1 Whittaker Street, Bolton and Thomas was working as a cotton warehouseman.

Name	Flanagan, Thomas
Rank	Lance Corporal
Number	16990
Unit	6th Bn The Loyal North Lancashire Regiment
Born	Bolton, Lancashire c.1887
Enlisted	Bolton, Lancashire
Died	Malta 25 September 1915
Age	28
Grave or Memorial	Addolorata Cemetery, Malta

Roland Foster

Bolton Journal and Guardian 1 October 1915

Horwich Soldier Killed in Action

Mrs. Foster, 4, Taylor-st. has received information from the War Office of the death of her son, **Pte. Roland Foster**, aged 22, of A Company, 6th Battalion Loyal North Lancashires in the Dardanelles. He enlisted on August 25th last year, and prior to that was a crane driver in the foundry in the Loco. Works. Mrs Foster is a widow and has two other sons in the Army, one, Pte. John Foster, being the twin brother of the dead hero, and is in the 1st Battalion, King's Own Royal Lancaster Regiment. He has been at the front for some time, and has been returned to duty after having been wounded.

Roland was the son of Thomas Foster and Ann Catherine (or Katherine) Foster née Jones b.1868.

Roland appeared on census returns as Rowland.

In 1901 Roland was living at 28 Heavily Grove, Horwich, with his mother and twin brother John and brothers Daniel b.1895 and Henry b.1898.

In 1911 Roland was living at 5 Short Street, Horwich with his by then widowed mother and brothers John, Daniel, Henry and James b.1906.

Roland was at that point employed as a general labourer in a paper works.

Name
Foster, Roland
Rank
Private
Number
11104
Unit
6th Bn The Loyal North Lancashire Regiment
Born
Rivington, Lancashire 1893
Enlisted
Bolton, Lancashire 25 August 1914
Died
Gallipoli, Turkey 27 August 1915
Age
22
Grave or Memorial
7th Field Ambulance Cemetery, Gallipoli, Turkey

Name
Fox, James

Rank
Private

Number
19732

Unit
6th Bn Border Regiment

Born
Bolton, Lancashire c.1885

Enlisted
Bolton, Lancashire January 1915

Died
Gallipoli, Turkey 30 April 1915

Age
30

Grave or Memorial
Helles Memorial, Gallipoli, Turkey

James Fox

Bolton Journal and Guardian 25 August 1916

It is over 12 months since **Pte. JAS. FOX**, Border Regiment, was reported "Missing" in the Gallipoli field of war, and on Tuesday the War office notified his wife that they were now "constrained to conclude that he is dead." Aged 30, and a labourer at Lum-st Gas Works, Fox leaves two children.

James was the son of Peter Fox b.1846, a hand car driver and Ellen Fox b.1853.

In 1891 James was living at 19 Back Acresfield, Bolton with his parents and siblings Catherine b.1875, William b.1881, Peter b.1883 and John J b.1885.

James married Jane Brown b.1885 at St George's Church, Bolton on 26 June 1909.

In 1911 the couple were living at 31 Craddock Street, Bolton with their sons, Harold b.1909 and William b.1910.

James was then working as a carter in the flour trade.

At the time of his enlistment in January 1915 his occupation was given as iron fixer.

Walter Freeman

A FIGHTING FAMILY

The Freemans, of 19 Merrick-st, are a family of fighters, four sons and the father having responded to the call. The father put in 21 years with the old Bolton Volunteers, and is now with the 5th King's Liverpool Regt., guarding prisoners on the Isle of Man. **Walter**, 19 years of age, joined the King's Own Scottish Borderers, and was drowned when the Royal Edward was torpedoed. Richard, 32 years of age, was in the fighting at Suvla Bay with the Lancashire Fusiliers, and was wounded in the right arm. He is now in hospital. Matthew is stationed at Edinburgh with the K.S.O.B. John is a bombardier with the Bolton Artillery at Bettisfield Park Camp, having served five years with that unit.

Walter lost his life alongside hundreds of others when HMT Royal Edward was torpedoed by the German submarine UB-14 while en route from Alexandria to Lemnos. The ship was carrying 1367 officers and men destined for Gallipoli.

Name	
	Freeman, Walter
Rank	
	Private
Number	
	11636
Unit	
	1st Bn King's Own Scottish Borderers
Born	
	Bolton, Lancashire c.1896
Enlisted	
	Ashton-under-Lyne
Died	
	At sea 13 August 1915
Age	
	19
Grave or Memorial	
	Helles Memorial, Gallipoli, Turkey

ABBOTT, WILLIAM W.	GRIME, ARTHUR
ASHWORTH, ALFRED T.	HALL, THOMAS
BARLOW, ARTHUR	HALLIWELL, GEORGE A.
BARLOW, JOSEPH	HALLIWELL, JAMES
BARLOW, ROBERT W.	HALLOWS, ERNEST
BELLIS, HERBERT	HAMPSON, JOHN R.
BLINKHORN, RICHARD	HANCOCK, JABEZ
BOARDMAN, EDWARD	HARDMAN, ARTHUR E.
BOARDMAN, WILLIAM	HARDMAN, JAMES
BROCKLEHURST, FRED	HEATON, JAMES
BROOKS, WILLIAM	HILL, ZACHARIAH
CHATTERLEY, WILLIAM	HINDLEY, HARRY
CROMPTON, STANLEY	HORNBY, RICHARD
DAVIES, J. ROBERT	JARVIS, JOHN
DUCKWORTH, ALBERT	JENKINSON, WILLIAM
DUXBURY, JAMES	KAY, WALTER
EDWARDS, JAMES	KING, JOHN
FISHWICK, CHARLES	KIRKMAN, GEORGE
FLETCHER, THOMAS	KIRKPATRICK, ISAAC
GREENHALGH, ALBERT	KIRKPATRICK, WILLEY

LOCKTON, THOMAS	SCHOLES, JESSE
LOWE, GEORGE	SETTLE, CYRIL
LYONS, JAMES	SETTLE, JAMES
MARTIN, CHARLES	SHARPLES, J. WILLIAM
MARTIN, THOMAS	SHARPLES, WILLIAM
MILLS, CHARLES	SHAW, JAMES
MORLEY, WILLIAM	SINGLETON, HARRY
MORRIS, ALFRED	SIVITER, WILLIAM
MORRIS, THOMAS	SIVITER, JOSEPH
MORT, ROGER	SIVITER, SAMUEL
NUTTALL, HARRY	SLADEN, HARRY
PARR, CHARLES	SMITH, NORMAN
PARRY, ROBERT T.	SWINGWOOD, GEORGE
PARTINGTON, ALBERT	TATLOCK, ROGER
PARTINGTON, WILLIAM	TAYLOR, HUBERT
PERCIVAL, WILLIAM	TAYLOR, JAMES
PLACE, ROBERT	TAYLOR, JOHN
ROBERTS, MATTHEW	WOOD, THOMAS
RYAN, EDWARD	WORSLEY, FRANK
SCHOLES, FRED	

Little Lever Memorial Library was opened on 17 August 1940 by **Lady Openshaw**, Chairman of Lancashire County Libraries.

The War Memorial itself is a tablet of Coniston sea green slate, the centre being a carved panel in Stancliffe stone. The sculptor was W H Doxey of Levenshulme. **Mr Seddon**, Trustee of the War Memorial Committee, said that 'although it was a little late in the day it was a suitable memorial to those men who gave their lives in the Great War'.

John Gannon

John's name appears on the Bolton Borough Roll of Honour.

Name	
	Gannon, John
Rank	
	Private
Number	
	2369
Unit	
	1st/8th Bn Manchester Regiment
Born	
Enlisted	
Died	
	Gallipoli, Turkey 8 July 1915
Age	
Grave or Memorial	
	Lancashire Landing Cemetery, Gallipoli, Turkey

Name	
Garner, Henry	
Rank	
Driver	
Number	
1049	
Unit	
1/1st (East Lancs)	
Battery	
Royal Field Artillery	
Born	
Bolton, Lancashire	
c.1894	
Enlisted	
Bolton, Lancashire	
9 October 1913	
Died	
Gallipoli, Turkey	
13 October 1915	
Age	
21	
Grave or Memorial	
Twelve Tree Copse Cemetery, Gallipoli, Turkey	

Henry Garner

Bolton Journal and Guardian 5 November 1915

Artillery Territorial Killed in Gallipoli

Col. Walker, who is in command of the Bolton Artillery in Gallipoli, reports the death on October 13th of **Driver Harry Garner**, who received a shot in the head. Driver Garner was 21 years of age, and formerly lived in lodgings in Craddock-st. He had been in the Artillery a number of years and went into camp with them at Turton in August, 1914, and later to Egypt. By trade he was a carter. Col. Walker states that he was a competent telephone linesman and a cheery comrade.

Bolton Journal and Guardian 26 November 1915

Bolton Men in Gallipoli. 18 Battery's First Death

On Wednesday, the 13th October, a casualty occurred that greatly affected the ranks. **Driver H. Garner** (1049), whilst on duty as wireman at the forward observation station, was killed during a fusillade of artillery and rifle fire. The bullet caused instantaneous death. "'Jerry' was the most light-hearted and best-tempered man in his battery, and his cheering laugh and lively song will be always remembered by his comrades. Driver Garner is the first of the 18th Battery to die for his King and country in the great cause. He was buried in the Georghegaris Bluff Cemetery on October 14th. The service was conducted by the Church of England chaplain and was attended by 40 officers, N.C.O.'s, and men. A cross was erected to his memory, and the spot will be reverenced by all."

On enlistment Henry had been working as a carter for Thomas Walmsley & Sons in Bolton.

His name is on the Bolton Artillery War Memorial in Nelson Square, Bolton.

Samuel Gee

Farnworth Weekly Journal 13 August 1915

DIED AT MALTA

Mr. Samuel Gee, of 12, Conway-st, Farnworth, on Monday week received a telegram stating that his son, **Private Samuel Gee**, of the R.A.M.C., was lying dangerously ill in Malta, and it was regretted that permission could not be granted to visit him. A few days later came the official intimation from the Record Office that the young soldier, who would have attained his 23rd year on Monday next, had died from dysentery on July 3rd*, and this was accompanied by Lord Kichener's letter conveying the condolences of the King and Queen. This week has come a letter from Private Sam Phoenix of the R.A.M.C., from the hospital at Malta, dated August 2nd. stating that Private Gee had passed away at 9-15 the same morning and that all that was possible had been done to save him. In spite of the best medical attention his life could not be saved. The deceased, who was a stripper at the Century Mills, New Bury, enlisted in January at the Town Hall, and after his training went to the Dardanelles about two months ago. His last letter home brought the news that he had landed in Alexandria. He attended St. James's School, New Bury, and was very well known and highly esteemed in that district.

Samuel was the son of Samuel Gee b.1866, a stonemason, and Esther Gee née Blinkhorn b.1871.

In 1901 his parents and baby brother Henry b.1900 were living at 4 Tong Row, Farnworth.

Samuel and his brother Robert b.1896 were staying a few doors away with the Brade family at 6 Tong Street.

Their sister, Elizabeth Ann b.1895, was staying next door to them at 2 Tong Street with the Ogden family.

Their other sister Sarah b.1899 was a patient at Farnworth Infection Hospital.

By the 1901 Census Samuel was living at 4 Tong Row with his parents and siblings Elizabeth Ann, Robert and Sarah.

Samuel was employed as a card tenter in a cotton mill.

His name is on Farnworth War Memorial.

* CWGC date of death is different from newspaper report, which is in itself contradictory.

Name	
	Gee, Samuel
Rank	
	Private
Number	
	50415
Unit	
	40th Field Ambulance Royal Army Medical Corps
Born	
	Horwich, Lancashire 1892
Enlisted	
	Farnworth, Lancashire January 1915
Died	
	Malta 31 July 1915
Age	
	22
Grave or Memorial	
	Pieta Military Cemetery, Malta

Stanley Gill

Bolton Journal and Guardian 11 February 1916

FOUR HORWICH BROTHERS - ONE KILLED

Information has been received by his brother, Mr. Wm. Gill,19, Lester-st, Horwich, that **Pte. Stanley Gill** (19), of the 4th Battalion, South Wales Borderers, was killed in action on the Gallipoli Peninsula. The hero joined the R.A.M.C. a month after the commencement of the war, but was later transferred to the South Wales Borderers, and went to the Dardanelles in November, 1915, after having been in training at Aldershot, Llandrindod Wells, and Liverpool. The first intimation Mr. Gill had was contained in a letter received from the soldier's brother, Pte. John Gill, 6th Battalion L.N.L., who is also with the Mediterranean Forces, in which he said "I am sorry to say our Stanley was killed in action on January 8th. There were six men and an officer, and they were all killed by a shell. The enemy then sent two more shells, which buried all of them, and they had to be dug out." A letter was subsequently received from Stanley's officer, Lieut. A. Buchanan, in which it was stated that death was instantaneous. At the time of enlisting Gill worked at the Firwood Bleachworks, but was previously employed in the boiler shop at the Horwich Loco. Works. He is one of six brothers, four of whom are in the Army. They are Pte. John, 6th Battalion L.N.L., at the Dardanelles, Pte. Paul L.N.L., in training at Felixstowe, and Pte. Tom, 10th battalion L.N.L., in France.

Stanley was the son of Thomas Gill b.1859, a labourer, and Elizabeth Gill b.1859.

His parents first appeared together on the 1881 Census where they were living in Horwich with sons Thomas b.1879 and John b.1880.

By 1891 the family were living at 1 Gorton Fold, Horwich. Thomas jnr had died but John had been joined by siblings William b.1883, Paul b.1885, Albert Edward b.1887 and Mary Hannah b.1889.

Stanley appeared on the Census for the first time in 1901, living at 5 Gorton Fold with his parents and siblings as above and brother Thomas b.1895. Thomas snr was listed working as a labourer at Horwich Loco Works.

Thomas Gill snr died in 1907. The 1911 Census recorded Stanley living with his mother, brother Thomas and nephew John Walter Gill b.1902 at 4 Tredgold Street, Horwich. Stanley was listed as being employed as an apprentice boilermaker at the Loco Works.

Name
Gill, Stanley
Rank
Private
Number
24671
Unit
4th Bn South Wales Borderers
Born
Horwich, Lancashire c.1896
Enlisted
Farnworth, Lancashire
Died
Gallipoli, Turkey 7 January 1916
Age
19
Grave or Memorial
Helles Memorial, Gallipoli, Turkey

William Glazebrook

Bolton Journal and Guardian 7 January 1916

Killed in Gallipoli

The War Office has notified Mrs. Glazebrook, 111, Leicester-st.,that her husband, **Pte. William Glazebrook**, 6th Loyal North Lancashire Regiment, has been killed in action in Gallipoli. Pte. Glazebrook, who was 39 years of age, and leaves a widow and seven children, enlisted on November 1st 1914. He was in training at Felixstowe, and went to Gallipoli in August of last year, and was killed on November 27th. Prior to enlisting he was employed in the Corporation Gas Department, and attended St. Matthew's Church. About 20 years ago he was for a short period in the Bolton Volunteers.

William was the son of William Glazebrook b.1839, a stone mason, and Mary Ellen Glazebrook b.1835.

He first appeared on the 1881 Census living with his parents and (much) older sister Alice b.1857 at 6 Westbury Street, Bolton.

In 1891 the family were living at 15 Draycott Street, Bolton and William jnr had started work as an apprentice gas fitter.

William's father died in 1892.

William married Elizabeth Ann Horrocks b.1877 at All Souls Church, Bolton on 13 February 1897.

The couple first appeared on the 1901 Census, living at 17 Draycott Street, next door to William's mother and sister Alice. They had two daughters: Doris b.1888 and Edith b.1889.

William was absent from the 1911 Census but his wife, Elizabeth Ann, was living at 12 Topping Street, Bolton with children Doris, Edith, Mary b.1902, Edna b.1905 and William b.1908. William and Elizabeth had two other children: Arthur b.1912 and Annie b.1914.

William's medical examination on enlisting in the Army recorded him as being 5' 5" tall and weighing 115 lbs, with grey eyes and brown hair.

Name
Glazebrook, William
Rank
Private
Number
4617
Unit
6th Bn The Loyal North Lancashire Regiment
Born
Bolton, Lancashire c.1876
Enlisted
Bolton, Lancashire 2 November 1914
Died
Gallipoli, Turkey 27 November 1915
Age
39
Grave or Memorial
Green Hill Cemetery, Gallipoli, Turkey

Name	
Glennerster, Wright	
Rank	
Private	
Number	
17794	
Unit	
1st Bn	
Border Regiment	
Born	
Atherton, Lancashire	
1896	
Enlisted	
Bolton, Lancashire	
January 1915	
Died	
Gallipoli, Turkey	
4 December 1915	
Age	
19	
Grave or Memorial	
Lancashire Landing Cemetery, Gallipoli, Turkey	

Wright Glennerster

Wright was the son of Frederick William Glennerster b.1866, a coal miner and sometime innkeeper, and Margaret Glennerster b.1868.

He first appeared on the 1901 Census living at 26 Mabel Street, Westhoughton with his parents and siblings Emily b.1888, Annie b.1889, Sarah b.1894, Elizabeth Ellen b.1898 and Albert b.1900.

By 1911 he was living at 2 Roundthorne, Westhoughton with his parents and siblings Emily, Annie, Sarah, Elizabeth, Albert, Margaret b.1907, Eveline b.1908 and Miriam b.1910.

Wright was then working as a tub drawer underground in a coal mine.

His name is on Westhoughton War Memorial.

Albert Graham

Bolton Journal and Guardian 13 August 1913

Another Dardanelles Hero

Pte (No/17864) **Albert Graham** R.M.L.I. was killed in action near the Dardanelles on August 3rd. This news was conveyed in a telegram from Alexandria to the authorities in London, who have forwarded the information to deceased father at 36, Rose-st. graham, who was not yet 19 years of age, enlisted on September 19th. Last year, and was in the Deal Battalion of Royal Marine Brigade of the Royal Naval Division. Prior to enlisting he was employed as a side-piecer at the No.2 mill of Messrs. Crosses and Winkworth Ltd., Rose Hill. He was connected with St. Mark's Church and Schools.

Albert was the son of Frederick Charles Graham b.1870, a spinning mule fitter, and Hannah Graham née Howarth b.1870.

On the 1901 Census Albert's parents were living at 43 Leach Street, Bolton with his sister, Lily b.1900.

4 year old Albert was in Hulton Fever Hospital, Bolton as a patient.

By 1911 the family were still living in the same house but with two additional children: Fred b.1903 and Ivy b.1906.

Name	
Graham, Albert	
Rank	
Private	
Number	
PO/17864	
Unit	
Portsmouth Bn Royal Naval Division, Royal Marine Light Infantry	
Born	
Bolton, Lancashire 31 Aug 1896	
Enlisted	
Manchester 19 September 1914	
Died	
Alexandria, Egypt 3 August 1915	
Age	
18	
Grave or Memorial	
Alexandria (Chatby) Military and War Cemetery, Egypt	

Victor Collins Green

GreenBolton Journal and Guardian 5 November 1915

Harwood Soldier Dies from Wounds

"Died from wounds" is the brief official notification received of the fate of **Private Victor C. Green**, of the Essex Regiment, who had been serving in the Dardanelles, the news having been forwarded to Mr. Samuel Scowcroft, Higher Barn Farm, Harwood, who had always taken a very deep interest in the lad. Green was left an orphan when only five years old, and was taken out of the Fishpool Institution by Mr. Scowcroft. He enlisted early this year in the R. F. A., and was stationed for some months at Newcastle. After wards he was moved to Harwich, where he was transferred to the Essex Regiment. He sailed for the Eastern theatre of war on Sept. 1st. The gallant soldier, who was only 18 years of age, was on the roll of honour at Harwood Church.

Victor was the son of Joseph Collins b.1862, an iron moulder.

He appeared on the 1901 Census living at 4 Thomas Street, Bury with his father and half sister Elizabeth E Collins b.1890.

Joseph died in 1903, leaving Victor an orphan. "Fishpool Institution" was the Bolton Workhouse on the site of what is now the Royal Bolton Hospital.

On the 1911 Census he was listed as a milk boy (dairy) / servant living with farmer Samuel Scowcroft, his wife Emma Scowcroft and brother Henry Scowcroft at Higher Barn Farm, Harwood.

Name	Green, Victor Collins
Rank	Private
Number	20178
Unit	1st Bn Essex Regiment
Born	Bury, Lancashire c.1897
Enlisted	Bolton, Lancashire
Died	Gallipoli, Turkey 5 October 1915
Age	18
Grave or Memorial	Helles Memorial, Gallipoli, Turkey

George Arthur Greenhalgh

Bolton Journal and Guardian 6 August 1915

BOLTON R.A.M.C. MAN KILLED AT GALLIPOLI

The first member of the 1st Lancashire Field Ambulance, which is the Bolton Territorial Section of the R.A.M.C., under Lieut.-Col. H. G. Parker, to lose his life, is **Pte. George Arthur Greenhalgh**, 135, Merehall-st., Bolton, who was wounded on July 10th and died the following day. Greenhalgh, who was 19 years of age, was employed as a book-keepr by Messrs. Burgons, Deansgate. He attended St. George's-rd. Congregational Church. Liet.-Col. Parker writes to say that deceased was on duty at one of the dressing stations when he was struck across the front of the body and arms by a huge Turkish shell. He was operated upon, but died on the following day and was buried near Cape Helles, where the men first arrived in the Gallipoli Peninsula. Lieut.-Col. Parker concludes: The whole of my men are deeply grieved at our loss. He was a good young lad, never grumbling at the heavy work he had to do. He was always ready to risk his life to help the wounded of the fighting forces of our division. Most of the work has fallen on the 1st Field Ambulance.

George was the son of Marcus Greenhalgh b.1864, a mineral water salesman, and Mary Greenhalgh née Smethurst b.1864.

George first appeared on the 1901 Census living at 22 Colwyn Grove, Bolton with his parents and sister Mary Jane b.1897. Another sister, Margaret Ethel b.1889 died in infancy.

In 1911 George was living at 133 Marshall Street, Bolton with his parents and sister Mary Jane.

He was then working as a clerk to a provision merchants.

Name	Greenhalgh, George Arthur
Rank	Private
Number	187
Unit	1st/1st East Lancs Field Ambulance Royal Army Medical Corps
Born	Bolton, Lancashire 1895
Enlisted	Bolton, Lancashire
Died	Gallipoli, Turkey 11 July 1915
Age	19
Grave or Memorial	Lancashire Landing Cemetery Gallipoli, Turkey

Name
Greenhalgh, Harold Joseph
Rank
Private
Number
11402
Unit
6th Bn The Loyal North Lancashire Regiment
Born
Egerton, Lancashire 28 March 1895
Enlisted
Bolton, Lancashire
Died
Gallipoli, Turkey 9 August 1915
Age
20
Grave or Memorial
Helles Memorial, Gallipoli, Turkey

Harold Greenhalgh

Bolton Journal and Guardian 17 September 1915

More 6th Lancashire Losses after Suvla Bay Landing

The eldest of the two soldier sons of Mr. and Mrs. Lawrence Greenhalgh, 2, Dimple, is officially posted as missing. **Private Harold Greenhalgh** was a member of the machine gun section attached to the 6th Battalion L.N.L. Regiment, and participated in the gallant charge of the battalion on August 9th. He was a fine soldier and at Tidworth was singled out for valet duties by Lieut. Grimshaw. He was employed at Messrs. Bridson's bleachworks, and formerly resided at Dunscar and Brookbank, Harwood. His brother, Private George Ashton Greenhalgh, is serving with the 9th battalion L.N.L. Regiment. The companion of Private Greenhalgh, Corporal Walker, of 34 Horrocks-st, Vallets, is also missing.

Harold was the son of Lawrence Greenhalgh b.1867, a cotton dyer, and Sarah Frances Greenhalgh née Ashton b.1869.

He was born as Joseph Harold Greenhalgh at 199 Darwen Road, Bromley Cross.

Harold (as Joseph Harold) appeared on the 1901 Census at 26 Egerton Vale, Egerton with his parents and siblings: George Ashton b.1893 and Ellen b.1897.

By the 1911 Census the family were living at 26 Edward Street, Bolton where the family now included three more children: Mabel b.1907, Mary b.1909 and Lawrence b.1910.

They moved again later to 2 Dimple, Egerton.

Harold attended school in Walmsley before going to work as a dyer at Bridson's bleachworks on Chorley Street, Bolton.

His name is on Dunscar War Memorial.

James Grogan

Bolton Journal and Guardian 3 September 1915

Maxim Gunner Killed in Gallipoli

News is to hand regarding the death in action at the Dardanelles of **Lance-Corporal James Grogan**, whose parents reside at 12, Eldon-st., Tonge Moor. He enlisted on Dec. 5th in the Royal Dublin Fusiliers, and after spending a few days in Ireland was sent to Sittingbourne, where he remained in training until May 14th. He was then drafted from Devonport to the Dardanelles. On landing he was entrusted with a Maxim gun, and it was whilst serving with this that he met with his death. His parents first received news of their son's death in a letter from a comrade. On Aug 3rd the news was verified by Pte. Joseph Kindred, also of Bolton, who has been twice wounded. It was not, however, until Aug. 24th. That official news was received. Deceased was a very highly respected member of St. Mary's, where he was head acolyte. This year was the first time for 17 years that he has failed to be present in the annual Catholic procession. He was 20 years of age, and was formerly employed as a side piecer at the Mill Hill No. 1 Mill. Sympathetic reference to the death was made at all services at St. Mary's on Sunday.

James was the son of James Grogan b.1871, a cotton spinner / self-actor minder, and Margaret Ellen Grogan née Flaherty b.1872.

In 1901 James was living at 62 Horsa Street, Bolton with his parents and brother Daniel b.1897 and Thomas b.1899.

By 1911 the family were living at 50 Pole Street, Bolton along with three additional children: Mary Teresa b.1902, Joseph b.1905 and Francis b.1908.

James jnr was by that time working as a piecer in a cotton mill.

Name	Grogan, James
Rank	Private
Number	17514
Unit	1st Bn Royal Dublin Fusiliers
Born	Bolton, Lancashire c.1895
Enlisted	Bolton, Lancashire
Died	Gallipoli, Turkey 12 July 1915
Age	20
Grave or Memorial	Twelve Tree Copse Cemetery, Gallipoli, Turkey

Albert Grundy

Bolton Journal and Guardian 23 July 1915

Ex-Militiaman Killed

Another Bolton hero who laid down his life in the gallant attempt which is being made to force the Dardanelles is **Private Albert Grundy**, of the 1st Border Regiment. His eldest sister has received notification to the effect that he died on July 5th from wounds received in the Dardanelles. Grundy was a single man, 27, and was formerly employed at the Horwich Loco Works. He has three sisters and one brother in Bolton and another brother, William, is at present with the Royal Field Artillery in Wiltshire. The deceased formerly worked with Mrs. Walker, Chorley Old-rd. For a number of years he was in the Militia and had been about three years on reserve when the war broke out. He was called up for service and stayed at Barrow-in-Furness until four months ago. He was then drafted to the Dardanelles and died as stated from wounds received.

Albert was the son of William Grundy b.1847, a steel forge labourer, and Sarah Grundy b.1851, a cotton weaver.

Albert first appeared on the 1891 Census living at 41 Forge Street. Bolton with his parents and siblings: James Robert b.1876, William b.1879 and Sarah b.1887. He also had two older sisters who had married and left home by that point: Mary Ellen b.1867 and Elizabeth b.1869.

His father died in 1900 and in 1901 Albert was living at 19 Buxton Street with his mother and sister Sarah. He was also - at the age of 11 - working as a cotton piecer (half timer).

On the 1911 census he appeared (incorrectly described as having been born in Oldham) living as a boarder in the household of Mrs Priscilla Walker at 19 Benson Street, Bolton and was working as a cotton doubler.

On enlistment in 1915 he was still living at 19 Benson Street. His occupation was given as castor maker. His medical examination records him as being 5' 3" tall.

His Army Service Record states that he was admitted to the 19th General Hospital, Alexandria, Egypt on 3 July 1915 having been wounded in action: shrapnel wounds to his right thigh, right eye and right axilla (armpit). He died from his injuries two days later.

His effects and medals were instructed to be sent to Miss Esther Duckworth b.1889 of 11 Benson Street, Bolton.

Albert's name is on the Horwich Loco Works War Memorial.

Name	
Grundy, Albert	
Rank	
Private	
Number	
19161	
Unit	
1st Bn Border Regiment	
Born	
Bolton, Lancashire 1888	
Enlisted	
Bolton, Lancashire 8 January 1915	
Died	
Alexandria, Egypt 5 July 1915	
Age	
27	
Grave or Memorial	
Twelve Tree Copse Cemetery, Gallipoli, Turkey	

Samuel Guffogg

Bolton Journal and Guardian 18 February 1916

Another Deane Hero Falls

Official intimation has been received by his parents, Mr. and Mrs. Guffogg, 117, Deane Church-lane, of the death of their son, **Bombardier Guffogg**, of the 1/3rd East Lancashire Brigade R.F.A. The deceased soldier served for some time with the Bolton Artillery (Territorials), and when the war broke out went with his battery to Turton. He was shortly after drafted to Egypt. Guffogg took part in all the fighting with the Bolton drafts. It was while returning from Gallipoli over what is known as the "V" beach, that he was struck with shrapnel, dying two days later. During the last battle on the Peninsula he received his promotion. Sergt. H. Parker, writing to his parents, says:- "I am very sorry to inform you that your son, Sam, was severely wounded by a shell on the night of the 8th of January as we were leaving our position. With myself and two gunners he had to stay behind to the last with our gun. For the time being we had been attached to a Regular Battalion of Horse Artillery. We had just got our gun ready for blowing up when a big howitzer shell pitched amongst us, knocking all of us off our feet. I found Sam was badly hit in both arms and right side, and two more men belonging to "Y" Battery were also hurt. That left myself and another comrade. We carried Sam down to the dressing station on Gully Beach, where we had to leave him. I cannot tell you if he was brought off the Peninsula, but I hope so. We had to hurry away at once to "W" Beach to embark, and were only just in time to catch our party, so that I cannot give you any further information. All his chums deeply sympathise with you, and we hope he will soon be restored to health. He bore up very bravely under his injuries, was quite conscious when we left him and bade us good-bye." Bombardier Guffogg was a fine specimen of young manhood, standing well over six feet, and proportionately built. In civil life he was a collier at Peel Hall Collieries, and had won several certificates in his calling. He had been for some time a Sunday schoolteacher at Peace-st. Mission, his name appearing No. 1 on the Roll of Honour at that place of worship, and, strange to say, he is the first to fall.

Samuel was the son of Albert Edward Guffogg b.1874, a collier / hewer, and Jane Ellen Guffogg née Bailey b.1874.

In 1901 Samuel was living at 118 Deane Church Lane with his parents, sister Mary b.1897 and brother Hamblet Harold b.1900.

On the 1911 Census he was living at 117 Deane Church Lane with his parents and siblings. His brother had settled for being known as plain Harold. At that point Samuel was employed as an apprentice joiner.

His medical examination on enlistment recorded him as being 5' 9" tall.

His Army record stated that he actually died at Kephalos on the island of Imbros from wounds received at Gallipoli the previous day. He was originally buried at Kephalos but the graves were transferred to the current site after the War.

His name is on the Bolton Artillery War Memorial in Nelson Square, Bolton.

Name	Guffogg, Samuel
Rank	Bombardier
Number	1044
Unit	1st/19th Battery 1st/3rd (East Lancs) Brigade Royal Field Artillery
Born	Bolton, Lancashire 1894
Enlisted	Bolton, Lancashire 12 September 1913
Died	Gallipoli, Turkey 9 January 1916
Age	22
Grave or Memorial	Lancashire Landing Cemetery, Gallipoli, Turkey

Arthur Hart

Bolton Journal and Guardian 1 December 1916

Another local man who enlisted on the outbreak of war and was lost in the Gallipoli fighting, and is now officially presumed to have died, is **Pte. ARTHUR HART**, Loyal North Lancashire Regiment. An employee in the making-up room at Gilnow Bleachworks, he lived with his parents at 27, Cross Ormrod-st., Bolton, and was 21 years of age. He set sail in July of last year, and was reported missing on August 8th. His name is on the St. Edmund's Roll of Honour.

Arthur was the son of Frederick Henry Hart b.1860, a cotton mill labourer, and Winifred Hart née Brady b.1859.

He first appeared on the Census in 1901 when he was living at 16 Bowden Street, Bolton with his parents and siblings Rosannah b.1879, Robert b.1883, Isabella b.1885, Frederick Henry b.1893 and Frank b.1897.

By 1911 the family were living at 94 Ellesmere Street, Bolton. Son Robert was no longer present but there was another daughter living there - Winifred b.1903 and a granddaughter Amelia Hart b.1905.

The 1911 Census records that Arthur was one of 11 children, 4 of whom had died by 1911.

He was at that point working as a plaiter down in a bleachworks.

Name	
Hart, Arthur	
Rank	
Private	
Number	
11918	
Unit	
6th Bn The Loyal North Lancashire Regiment	
Born	
Bolton, Lancashire 1895	
Enlisted	
Bolton, Lancashire	
Died	
Gallipoli, Turkey 9 August 1915	
Age	
20	
Grave or Memorial	
Helles Memorial, Gallipoli, Turkey	

Thomas Ardill Haslam

Thomas was the son of Samuel Haslam b.1864, a paviour's labourer, and Letitia Haslam née Ardill b.1863.

Thomas first appeared on the 1901 Census living at 124 Bark Street, Bolton with his parents and siblings Emma b.1895, Mary Ellen b.1897 and Percy b.1900. His mother was listed as being a grocer / shopkeeper.

Thomas's mother Letitia died in 1908.

In 1911 Samuel was still living at 124 Bark Street with children Mary Ellen, Percy and Charles Edward b.1904.

Thomas was already a private soldier serving with the Lancashire Fusiliers at their barracks in South Tidworth, Hampshire.

Name	
Haslam, Thomas Ardill	
Rank	
Private	
Number	
2210	
Unit	
1st Bn	
Lancashire Fusiliers	
Born	
Bolton, Lancashire	
1892	
Enlisted	
Bury, Lancashire	
Died	
Gallipoli, Turkey	
6 May 1915	
Age	
23	
Grave or Memorial	
Helles Memorial	
Gallipoli, Turkey	

Arthur Ellis Hardman

Farnworth Weekly Journal 24 September 1915

LITTLE LEVER SOLDIER MISSING

Mrs. Hardman of 108, Church-st, Little Lever, has received official intimation that her husband, **Pte. A. Ellis Hardman** (9519) 9th Lancashire Fusiliers, has been missing since August 21st. he was fighting at the Dardanelles. Although residing at Little Lever, Private Hardman was, in civil life, engaged at the Clifton Hall Colliery of Messrs. Knowles on the boundary of Swinton. He enlisted in November. His wife and four children are anxiously awaiting further news. In his last letter to his wife he states: "I am all right up to now, but we have had a hard time of it. We have just come out of the trenches for a rest. We were the first to land on this island, and the Turks have kept up a more or less continuous fire since. We we landed at first we made them run, and were at it for about four days. We shall get right with them some day. I shall never forget the night we landed. It was awful." Almost the last request Private Hardman made his wife was for a copy of the "Journal."

Arthur was the son of Ellis Hardman b.1842, a stonemason turned beerseller, and Martha Hardman née Lonsdale b.1839.

Arthur first appeared on the 1881 Census living at 96 Church Street, Little Lever with his parents and siblings Betsy b.1863, Esther Ann b.1865, Joseph b.1868, Lily b.18701, Sarah b.1873 and John b.1876.

In 1891 he was living at 56 Church Street (what is now the New Inn), Little Lever with his parents and siblings Esther Ann, Joseph, Lily, Sarah, John and Wilfred b.1882.

Arthur's father, Ellis, died in 1892.

By 1901 Arthur (listed as Ellis) was living with his mother and brother Wilfred at 8 Dearden Street, Little Lever. At this point Arthur was working as a coal miner / wagoner.

Arthur married Isabella Morley b.1882 on 11 June 1902 at St Matthew's Church, Little Lever.

Wilfred died in July 1902.

In 1911 the couple were living at 130 Church Street, Little Lever with their daughters Martha b.1904, Elizabeth b.1908 and Mary b.1909.

Arthur was working as a carter in 1911.

Two other children were recorded as having died by 1911, one being Ellis Hardman b.1906 who died aged 4 months.

The couple had two other children - Betsy b.1911 (who lived for just 28 days) and Alice b.1913.

Arthur's mother, Martha, died in December 1911.

His name is on Little Lever War Memorial.

James Hatton

James was the son of Edward Hatton b.1862, a machine iron turner, and Mary Hatton née Osborne b.1861.

James first appeared on the 1891 Census living at 37 Andrew Street with his parents and brothers John Joseph b.1882 and William Henry b.1883.

In 1901 the family were living at 50 Irving Street, Bolton with the addition of daughter Elizabeth b.1893. By this point James was working as a plaiter down in a bleachworks.

William Henry was married with a family of his own by 1911.

On the 1911 Census Elizabeth was living in the Catholic Girls' Home in Clarence Street, Bolton - not an institution but respectable accommodation run by the adjoining Convent for girls who would have been homeless otherwise. She was also employed as a laundress at the home.

Name	
	Hatton, James
Rank	
	Private
Number	
	11507
Unit	
	6th Bn The Loyal North Lancashire Regiment
Born	
	Bolton, Lancashire c.1886
Enlisted	
	Bolton, Lancashire
Died	
	Gallipoli, Turkey 9 August 1915
Age	
	29
Grave or Memorial	
	Helles Memorial, Gallipoli, Turkey

Name
Hewitt, Thomas
Rank
Private
Number
20076
Unit
1st Bn
Essex Regiment
Born
Horwich, Lancashire
1894
Enlisted
Royton, Lancashire
Died
Gallipoli, Turkey
7 October 1915
Age
21
Grave or Memorial
Helles Memorial,
Gallipoli, Turkey

Thomas Hewitt

Thomas was the son of Thomas Henry Hewitt b.1863, a machinist and joiner's sawyer, and Mary Alice Hewitt née Strickland b.1868.

Thomas first appeared on the 1901 Census living at 19 Winter Street, Horwich with his parents and sisters Mary Ellen b.1890, Ethel b.1893 and Alice b.1901.

In 1911 he was living at 74 Bull Lane, Off Lever Street, Bolton with his parents and sisters Mary Ellen and Ethel. Alice and two other children had died by 1911.

Thomas was then working as a piler in an iron forge. His father was not working at the time of the Census.

James Hilton

James's name appears on the Bolton Borough Roll of Honour.

Name	
Hilton, James	
Rank	
Private	
Number	
2613	
Unit	
10th Bn Manchester Regiment	
Born	
c.1890	
Enlisted	
Died	
Gallipoli, Turkey 15 November 1915	
Age	
18	
Grave or Memorial	
Azmak Cemetery, Suvla, Gallipoli, Turkey	

| Name |
| Walter Hilton |
| Rank |
| Private |
| Number |
| 18410 |
| Unit |
| 6th Bn King's Own (Royal Lancaster Regiment) |
| Born |
| Chequerbent, Bolton, Lancashire c.1878 |
| Enlisted |
| Atherton, Lancashire |
| Died |
| Gallipoli, Turkey 28 September 1915 |
| Age |
| 37 |
| Grave or Memorial |
| Hill 10 Cemetery, Gallipoli, Turkey |

Walter Hilton

Walter was the son of William Hilton b.1835 and Diana Hilton b.1843

Walter married Elizabeth Dootson b.1880 at St James's Church, Westhoughton in 1900.

In 1901 they were living at 632 Manchester Road, Westhoughton.

By the 1911 Census they were living at 661 Manchester Road, Chequerbent, Westhougton with their children Betsy b.1902, Bertha b.1904, Ellen b.1906, Dinah b.1908 and James b.1910. They also looked after Walter's nephew Harry Hilton b.1907 and niece Mary Elizabeth Stevenson b.1897 - and they had a lodger, Walter's cousin William Hilton b.1874.

Walter worked as a coal miner hewer.

He died of wounds recieved at Gallipoli.

His name is on Westhoughton War Memorial.

THE KING'S OWN

William Hodgkinson

Bolton Journal and Guardian 10 September 1915

Lost with the Royal Edward

Several Boltonians were on board the Royal Edward when she was torpedoed and sunk in the Mediterranean on the 13th August...

Mrs. Hodgkinson, 5, Rock-st., Halliwell, has received intimation that her husband, **Private William Hodgkinson**, is among the missing from the sunken transport, Royal Edward. He enlisted in the R.A.M.C. in January, but after training in Wales, he was sent to Liverpool, and transferred to the South Wales Borderers. Pte Hodgkinson, who was 31 years of age, and leaves a wife and one child, worked at Messrs. Henry Bessemer's Forge and was on the roll of honour at the Cable-st. Wesleyan Mission.

William was the son of William Hogkinson b.1838, a labourer, and Selina Hodgkinson b.1839.

William first appeared on the 1891 Census living at 67 School Hill, Bolton with his mother and siblings Samuel b.1873 and Ellen b.1876. His father was not present.

William and Selina had at least five other children: Caroline b.1860, Levi b.1862, John b.1867. Sarah b.1869, and Margaret Ellen b.1871.

In 1901 William was living with his mother at 53 Halliwell Road with his mother (listed as Sophia) and was working as a pony driver in a coal pit.

William married Isabella Croston b.1889 at St Mark's Church, Bolton on 8 January 1910.

The couple appeared on the 1911 Census living at 5 Rock Street, Bolton with their daughter Selina b.1910.

William was employed as a steel forge worker.

His name appears on the Bolton Borough Roll of Honour.

He lost his life alongside hundreds of others when HMT Royal Edward was torpedoed by the German submarine UB-14 while en route from Alexandria to Lemnos. The ship was carrying 1367 officers and men destined for Gallipoli.

Name	Hodgkinson, William
Rank	Private
Number	24764
Unit	4th Bn South Wales Borderers
Born	Bolton, Lancashire 1884
Enlisted	Bolton, Lancashire January 1915
Died	Gallipoli, Turkey 13 August 1915
Age	31
Grave or Memorial	Helles Memorial, Gallipoli, Turkey

Harry Hogg

Harry's name appears on the Bolton Borough Roll of Honour.

Arthur Holden

Bolton Journal and Guardian 1 October 1915

Horwich Sergeant Killed

The Roll of Honour for Horwich is increasing rapidly. Information has been received of the death in Gallipoli on August 7th, of **Sergt. A. Holden**, 1/5th Lancashire Fusiliers. He was 23 years of age, and previous to being called up was employed at Messrs. W. E. Taylor and Co.'s Victoria Mills, Horwich, residing with Mr. Riley at 12, Scholes Bank. Deceased was a native of Bury, where his mother resides at 8, York-terrace, Wash-lane.

Name	
	Holden, Arthur
Rank	
	Sergeant
Number	
	484
Unit	
	1st/5th Bn Lancashire Fusiliers
Born	
	Bury, Lancashire c.1892
Enlisted	
	Bury, Lancashire
Died	
	Gallipoli, Turkey 7 August 1915
Age	
	23
Grave or Memorial	
	Helles Memorial, Gallipoli, Turkey

Name	
Holden, William Henry	
Rank	
Private	
Number	
18089	
Unit	
1st Bn	
Royal Dublin Fusiliers	
Born	
Farnworth, Lancashire	
c.1891	
Enlisted	
Farnworth, Lancashire	
2 January 1915	
Died	
Gallipoli, Turkey	
17 June 1915	
Age	
24	
Grave or Memorial	
East Mudros Military	
Cemetery,	
Lemnos, Greece	

William Henry Holden

Bolton Journal and Guardian

Killed in the Dardanelles

Mrs. Holden, of 157, Ellesmere-st., Farnworth, has been officially notified that her husband, **Pte. W. H. Holden**, of the 1st Batt. Royal Dublin Fusiliers, died of wounds whilst serving with the Mediterranean Forces on June 17th. he joined on January 2nd and did his training in Sittingbourne, Kent, previous to being drafted to the Dardanelles. He leaves a widow and three children. He served his time as a clogger with Mr. Martin Wolfendale, of Albert-rd., Farnworth, after which he took a shop of his own at the junction of Albert-rd. and Longcauseway. He was connected with St James's School and church.

William was the son of William James Holden b.1866, a timber sawyer, and Catherine Holden née Hope b.1866.

William first appeared on the 1891 Census living with his parents at 6 Albert Place, Farnworth

By 1901 they had moved to 37 Albert Place, Farnworth.

William James Holden died in 1903.

William's mother Catherine married Benjamin Jones Hughes in 1909.

William married Ann Watson b.1887 at St Peter's Church, Farnworth in 1909.

In 1911 they were living at 161 Ellesmere Street, Farnworth with their daughter Mary Elizabeth b.1910.

He was employed as a journeyman clogger.

They had three other children: William b.1911, George b.1913 and Wilfred b.1915.

William Hollas

Bolton Journal and Guardian 28 January 1916

Cotton Manufacturer's Son Killed

Mr. William Hollas, Seafield Road, Lytham, is informed by the Admiralty that his youngest son, **William**, was killed in action at the Dardanelles on December 27th. Deceased, who was 19 years of, belonged to the Public Schools Company of the Hawke Battalion, 1st Royal Naval Brigade. He was educated at Farnworth Grammar School and the King Edward School, Lytham, and was, up to enlisting last February, in the firm of Hollas, Ltd. cotton manufacturers, Bolton. He had been at the Dardanelles since May. The young hero was of a particularly bright and cheery disposition, and won the high regard of all with whom he came into contact, both in civil and naval life. The flag was flown at half-mast at the Mather-st Mills.

William was the son of William Hollas b.1856, cotton cloth manufacturer, and Alice Hollas née Nuttall b.1860.

In 1901 William was living at 44 Church Road, Kearsley with his parents and siblings: Florence b.1882, Arthur b.1885, Joseph b.1867, Alice b.1889, Hannah Louisa b.1895 and Jane b.18989.

Florence married Abraham Lomax in 1905.

By the 1911 Census the rest of the family were living at 9 Seafield Road, Lytham, Lancashire. They employed one live-in domestic servant.

William attended Farnworth Grammar School and was on the War Memorial there until the school was demolished after closing in 1982.

Name	
Hollas, Wiliam	
Rank	
Able Seaman	
Number	
London Z/1408	
Unit	
Hawke Bn Royal Naval Division	
Born	
Bolton, Lancashire 29 December 1896	
Enlisted	
Died	
Gallipoli, Turkey 27 December 1915	
Age	
19	
Grave or Memorial	
Helles Memorial, Gallipoli, Turkey	

Ralph Horne

Bolton Journal and Guardian 7 January 1916

Killed in Gallipoli

Word has been received by his mother at 56, Ashburner-st., that **Pte. Ralph Horne** (18,762), 6th Loyal North Lancashire Regiment, has been killed in action at a place not stated, on Nov. 27th. The deceased soldier, who was 22 years of age, enlisted in December of last year in the 3rd Loyal North Lancashire Regiment. In August of this year he was transferred to the 6th L.N.L., and immediately went to Gallipoli with them. He was in training at Felixstowe. When he enlisted he was working with his mother as a fruiterer, prior to which he had been a collier.

Ralph was the son of Ralph Horne b.1855, a fruit seller / greengrocer, and Alice Horne née Gregson b.1863, also a greengrocer by trade.

Ralph snr had been married prior to marrying Alice in 1893 and had two children from the earlier relationship: Harriet b.1880 and Charles b.1884.

In 1901 Ralph was living at 3 Hope Street, Wigan with his parents, half-brother Albert b.1890 (Alice's son - born Albert Gregson), brother Harold b.1895 and sister Mary Elizabeth b.1900. The family also employed a live-in domestic servant.

There had been two other children born to the couple: Ernest b.1893 and Harold's twin sister Rosanna who had both died in infancy.

Ralph's father died in 1905.

In 1911 he was living with his mother and brothers Harold and Edward b.1903 in Tunstall, Staffordshire (Where Ralph's father had been born).

Ralph and Harold were working as coal miners at the time.

Name	
Horne, Ralph	
Rank	
Private	
Number	
18762	
Unit	
6th Bn The Loyal North Lancashire Regiment	
Born	
Wigan, Lancashire 1893	
Enlisted	
Bolton, Lancashire	
Died	
Gallipoli, Turkey 27 November 1915	
Age	
22	
Grave or Memorial	
Green Hill Cemetery, Gallipoli, Turkey	

Samuel Horrocks

Bolton Journal and Guardian 30 June 1916

A Fusilier Hero

A native of Bolton, though latterly resident in Bury, **Pte. Samuel Horrocks**, Lancashire Fusiliers, who was officially posted as missing on June 6th, 1915, is this week reported to have died in action. Horrocks had no parents and was better known as Jopson, Mr. and Mrs. Jopson, 20, Bolton-st., Bury, having adopted him in infancy. Some years ago they conducted a business in the Tonge Moor and Chorley Old-rd. districts, where Horrocks was a familiar figure. His sister resides at 10, Percy-st., Bolton, where the news of his death was conveyed.

Samuel was the son of John Horrocks b.1854 and Emma Horrocks née Hoyle b.1854.

Samuel first appeared on the 1891 Census living at 28 Nottingham Street, Bolton with his widowed mother and his siblings Zilpha b.1879, George H b.1880, Alfred b.1886 and Herbert b.1900. The family were lodging with another widow and her children bringing the total to 12 people living in a 4 room house.

His adoptive parents were Philip Jopson, an ice cream manufacturer and sometime brush maker, and Sarah Jane Jopson.

On 1901 Census he was listed as Samuel Horrocks living with the Jopson family as their son at 133 Chorley Old Road, Bolton.

By the 1911 Census he was living at 40 Princess Street, Bury with the Jopson family. He was listed as Samuel Horrocks (a boarder - not son) and was working as a shop assistant (probably in the Jopson family business).

Name	
	Horrocks, Samuel
Rank	
	Private
Number	
	2185
Unit	
	1st/5th Bn Lancashire Fusiliers
Born	
	Bolton, Lancashire c.1883
Enlisted	
	Bury, Lancashire
Died	
	Gallipoli, Turkey 6 June 1915
Age	
	32
Grave or Memorial	
	Helles Memorial, Gallipoli, Turkey

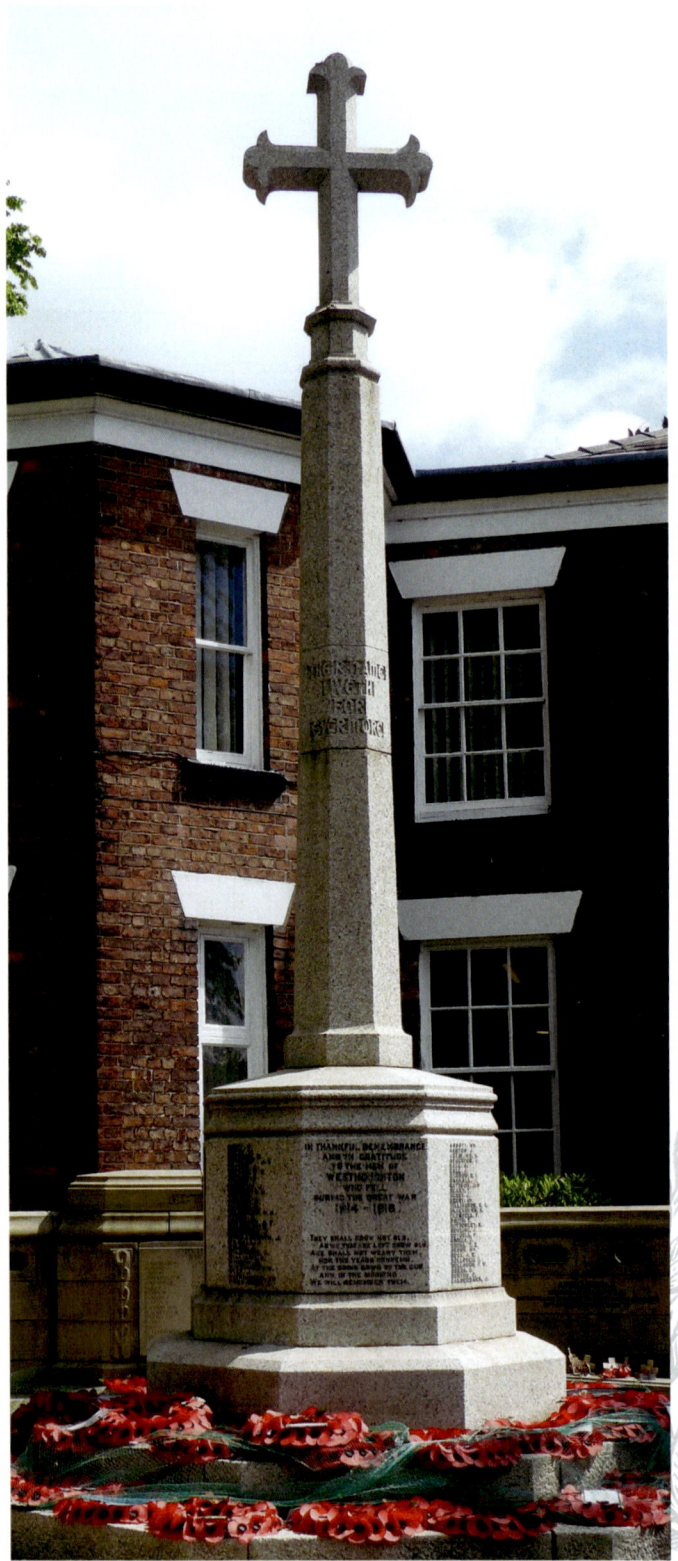

Edward Houghton

Edward's name appears on the Bolton Borough Roll of Honour.

Name	
	Houghton, Edward
Rank	
	Private
Number	
	1427
Unit	
	1st Bn
	Lancashire Fusiliers
Born	
	c.1879
Enlisted	
Died	
	Gallipoli, Turkey
	25 April 1915
Age	
	36
Grave or Memorial	
	Helles Memorial,
	Gallipoli, Turkey

Westhoughton War Memorial (left) was unveiled by Colonel Crosfield on 3 August 1923.

Kearsley War Memorial (far left) is in front of the now demolished Kearsley Town Hall on Bolton Road. It was dedicated in October 1921.

Name
Howard, Andrew
Rank
Private
Number
16477
Unit
6th Bn
The Loyal North
Lancashire Regiment
Born
Bolton, Lancashire
1895
Enlisted
Bolton, Lancashire
4 September 1914
Died
Gallipoli, Turkey
6 September 1915
Age
19
Grave or Memorial
Helles Memorial,
Gallipoli, Turkey

Andrew Howard

Andrew was the son of John Howard b.1871, a labourer. and Elizabeth Howard née Joynson b.1870.

He first appeared on the 1901 Census living at 10 Flash Street, Bolton with his parents and siblings Margaret Ann b.1889, Mary Ellen b.1890 and William b.1900.

Andrew's father died in 1909.

By the 1911 Census Andrew was living at 40 Partridge Street with his mother and siblings Margaret, Mary Ellen, James b.1906 and Elizabeth b.1909.

Andrew was working as a little piecer in a cotton mill.

His mother was recorded as having had 12 children, 6 of whom had died by 19111.

Andrew gave his occupation as carter when he enlisted in the Army.

His medical examination at the time recorded him as being 5' 3" tall, weighing 111 lbs and having a fresh complexion, blue eyes and light brown hair.

He appears to have died on board the Hospital Ship 'Beltan' in Mudros Bay from gunshot wounds to the thigh.

Frederick Howarth

Bolton Journal and Guardian 28 January 1916

A Missing Soldier

Private Frederick Howarth, who was serving in the Dardanelles, has been missing since August 9th, 1915, and his parents, who live at 51, Noble-st., have been officially notified of the fact. Many inquiries have been made at various Red Cross Hospitals, but no definite news has been received as to his whereabouts, and his parents would be glad to hear any news about him. The missing soldier is 20 years of age, and prior to enlisting he was employed at the Derby-st. Spinning Company's mill. His name is on the Fletcher-st. Weslyan School Roll of Honour.

Bolton Journal and Guardian 8 December 1916

Pte. FRED HOWARTH, L.N.L. Regiment, of 51, Noble-st., Bolton, was reported missing on August 9th. 1915, and is now reported to have been killed on that date.

Frederick was the son of Frederick Howarth b.1856, a forge labourer, and Theresa Howarth née Keeley b.1859.

He first appeared on the 1901 Census living at 82 Shaw Street, Bolton with his parents and siblings Ada b.1883, John b.1887, Catherine (Kate) b.1889, Henry b.1891 and Mary Alice b.1898. he also had an older sister Elizabeth Alice b.1880 who had died.

On the 1911 Census he was listed as living at 51 Noble Street, Bolton with his parents and siblings.

With the exception of his mother, the entire family were employed in the textile industry.

Frederick himself was working in a cotton spinning room.

Name	
	Howarth, Frederick
Rank	
	Private
Number	
	17770
Unit	
	6th Bn The Loyal North Lancashire Regiment
Born	
	Bolton, Lancashire c.1895
Enlisted	
	Bolton, Lancashire
Died	
	Gallipoli, Turkey 9 August 1915
Age	
	20
Grave or Memorial	
	Helles Memorial, Gallipoli, Turkey

Samuel Hulme

Bolton Journal and Guardian 10 September 1915

Boltonians in Fierce Engagement

NORTH LANCASHIRE MEN MISSING IN GALLIPOLI

Our photograph is of **Lance-Corporal Hulme** of the 8th L.N.L. Regiment, reproduced from a group of officers and N.C. O.'s when the battalion was training at Blackdown before proceeding to the Mediterranean, Hulme was only 19 years of age when he joined the Army, and we regret to say his mother at 3, Scott-st., Halliwell, has received the melancholy news that he was killed in action while gallantly serving his King with the Mediterranean Force in the Gallipoli Peninsular. He sailed for the Mediterranean in June, and had only been fighting a comparatively short time when he met his death on August 9th. He was a smart young soldier, and was quickly rewarded for his ability with his first stripe. He was a scholar at St. Matthew's School, and prior to joining the Army was a piecer at Park Mill, Gaskell-st.

Samuel was the son of Samuel Hulme b.1873, an iron moulder, and Emma Hulme née Bowker b.1874.

The 1901 Census showed Samuel as living at 8 Livingstone Street - the home of his maternal grandmother Elizabeth Bowker -with his mother and brother William Edward b.1895. his father was not present.

By 1911 Samuel was living with his mother and siblings William Edward, Albert b.1904, James b.1906. Alice b.1909. and Emma b.1910.

Samuel was working as a piecer. His father was once again not listed with them.

Two other children were recorded as having died by 1911. The family were boarding at 3 Scott Street in the household of James Seddon, a widower, and his daughter.

Name	Greenhalgh, Harold
Rank	Lance Corporal
Number	13852
Unit	6th Bn The Loyal North Lancashire Regiment
Born	Bolton, Lancashire c.1896
Enlisted	Bolton, Lancashire
Died	Gallipoli, Turkey 9 August 1915
Age	19
Grave or Memorial	Helles Memorial, Gallipoli, Turkey

Andrew Jackson

Bolton Journal and Guardian 24 September 1915

His Life for His Country

Many Boltonians have sacrificed their lives while fighting with the 6th L.N.L. Regiment at the Dardanelles, and the latest who has fallen in action is **Pte. Andrew Jackson**, whose mother lives at 51, Green-st. The gallant soldier, who was killed on August 30th, was only 20 years of age. Prior to the war he was a moulder at Messrs. Dobson and Barlow's Works. Four days before he met his heroic death he wrote home:- "I hope you are keeping your heart up, for I think it won't be long before this war is over. It is just a year ago since I 'listed."

James was the son of Mary Jackson b.1865.

On the 1911 Census Andrew was living at 51 Green Street, Bolton with his widowed mother and siblings James b.1893, Mary E b.1898, Bertha b.1902 and Florence b.1906.

Andrew's occupation was given as flyer maker.

His medical examination on enlistment record him as being 5' 4 5/8" tall and weighing 104 lbs with blue eyes and brown hair.

In May 1915, while already enlisted in the Loyals, he attempted to "fraudulently enlist" again in the Royal Field Artillery (the Bolton Artillery) but was discovered.

His mother remarried in 1917 to Charles Eccles.

Name	
Jackson, Andrew	
Rank	
Private	
Number	
3247	
Unit	
6th Bn	
The Loyal North Lancashire Regiment	
Born	
Bolton, Lancashire	
c.1895	
Enlisted	
Bolton, Lancashire	
26 August 1914	
Died	
Gallipoli, Turkey	
30 August 1915	
Age	
20	
Grave or Memorial	
Green Hill Cemetery,	
Gallipoli, Turkey	

John Jarvis

John was the son of John Jarvis b.1849, a labourer in a chemical works and former coal miner, and Edith Jarvis née Cooke b.1862.

John first appeared on the 1891 Census living at 13 Clay Street, Farnworth with his parents.

By the 1901 Census he was living at 32 Elizabeth Street, Farnworth with his parents and brother Richard b.1896.

In 1911 John was living at 52 Devon Street, Farnworth as a boarder with his father in the household of Mary Isherwood.

John was at that time employed as a ballast man on the Lancashire and Yorkshire Railway.

John married Clara Lindley b.1891 on 9 August 1913 at St Matthew's Church, Little Lever.

They had one daughter, Edith b.1913.

His name is on the Lancashire and Yorkshire Railway War Memorial on Victoria Station, Manchester and also on Little Lever War Memorial.

Name	
	Jarvis, John
Rank	
	Private
Number	
	3329
Unit	
	1st Bn Lancashire Fusiliers
Born	
	Farnworth, Lancashire 1891
Enlisted	
	Bury, Lancashire
Died	
	Gallipoli, Turkey 25 April 1915
Age	
	24
Grave or Memorial	
	Helles Memorial, Gallipoli, Turkey

John Scotson Jones

Bolton Journal and Guardian 2 July 1915

Heroic Deane Soldier

The Rev. Arthur Lamb, of Deane, writes:- Private **John S. Jones**, R.M.L.I., late of Windy Hough, Deane Avenue, was killed in action at the Dardanelles on June 7th. He was a bright, genial young fellow, of a frank and winsome disposition. In enlisting at the beginning of the war he was actuated by a high sense of duty. His bright Christian character made him a favourite with all who knew him. He was actively associated with the Deane Congregational Church and Sunday School, being a teacher in the Primary Department. He will be greatly missed and deeply lamented, but his influence and memory will ever be an inspiration to those who knew him. There was in him much of the "stuff of which heroes are made." He was employed at Messrs. R. Entwistle and Co., Lincoln Mills Warehouse.

John was the son of John Owen Jones b.1864, a provision dealer, and Sarah Jones née Scotson b.1870.

In 1901 John was living at Brighton Cottages, Rhyl, Flintshire with his parents and brothers James Hugh b.1894, Ernest Owen b.1896, Herbert Scotson b.1899, Harold Scotson b.1901.

John's father and brother Harold Scotson Jones both died in 1905.

His mother remarried in 1909 to Thomas Edward Johnson b.1853, a stationer and newsagent.

On the 1911 Census John was living at 259 Deane Church Lane, Bolton with his mother, step-father and siblings James Hugh, Harold and Mary Scotson b.1903.

Name	
	Jones, John Scotson
Rank	
	Private
Number	
	PO/697(S)
Unit	
	Plymouth Bn Royal Naval Division, Royal Marine Light Infantry
Born	
	Rhyl, Flintshire 1898
Enlisted	
	Manchester 19 October 1914
Died	
	Gallipoli, Turkey 7 June 1915
Age	
	17
Grave or Memorial	
	Redoubt Cemetery, Helles, Gallipoli, Turkey

Name
Jones, Richard

Rank
Sapper

Number
Deal/1149(S)

Unit
Royal Marines
3rd Field Company,
Divisional Engineers,
Royal Naval Division

Born
Bolton, Lancashire
c.1889

Enlisted
9 February 1915

Died
Gallipoli, Turkey
22 July 1915

Age
26

Grave or Memorial
Helles Memorial,
Gallipoli, Turkey

Richard Jones

Bolton Journal and Guardian 20 August 1915

Daubhill Sapper Killed

Lieut-Commander A. Randall Wells, R.N.V.R., has notified Mrs. Helen Jones, 45, Dijon-st., Daubhill, that her husband, **Sapper Richard Jones** (1149) of the Royal Naval Division, was killed in action in Gallipoli on July 22nd. Before enlisting Jones was in the employ of Messrs. Walsh, plumbers, St.Helens-rd., and was held in the highest esteem by members of his society, of which he was the President. He was on the Roll of Honour of St. Philip's, and was for many years connected with the Mawdsley-st. P.S.A. Brotherhood*.

Richard was the son of Henry Jones b.1858, a coal miner and sometime railway worker, and Mary Edwards Jones née Boulton b.1858.

Richard appeared on the 1891 Census living at 54 Philip Street, Bolton with his parents and brothers Charles b.1886 and Harry b.1891.

In 1901 he was living at 62 Adelaide Street, Bolton with his parents and siblings Charles, Harry, Mary b.1893 and Robert b.1894.

By 1911 the family were living at 72 Randal Street, Bolton.

Richard was working as a steam pipe fitter.

Richard married Helen Hawkes at St Philip's Church, Bolton in 1912.

She remarried in 1917 to Jesse Aldred.

* *PSA = Pleasant Sunday Afternoon*

Thomas Kelly

Bolton Journal and Guardian 15 October 1915

His Life for his Country

The thread of hope held by Mrs. Kelly, 3, Livingstone-st., Brownlow Fold, for the safety of her son, **Corpl. Thos. Kelly**, has now been snapped by the official announcement that he is killed. Sometime ago Mrs. Kelly was told by a friend whose son had written home, saying that Kelly had died for his country. As the War Office only stated that he was missing it was hoped he might be a prisoner of war. When war broke out Kelly, who had been a colliery drawer at Deane, had been on the reserve, and after mobilization he was stationed with his regiment at Barrow-in-Furness. He left England for the Dardanelles about the middle of July, and had been in the fighting line about a month. His father is also in the army, having joined the Cheshire "Bantams" Regiment, and is in training with his battalion in Wiltshire.

Thomas was the son of Thomas Kelly b.1875, a machine moulder, and Elizabeth Kelly née Carr b.1876.

Thomas first appeared on the 1901 Census living at 6 Hunt Street, Bolton with his parents and sisters Margaret b.1895, Catherine b.1897 and Mary b.1901.

By the 1911 Census the family were living at 25 Irving Street, Bolton. Mary had died in infancy but there were three more children recorded - John b.1903, Ann b.1905 and Francis b.1910.

Thomas was at that time employed as a crofter in a bleachworks.

Name
Kelly, Thomas
Rank
Corporal
Number
3694
Unit
1st Bn Lancashire Fusiliers
Born
Bolton, Lancashire c.1896
Enlisted
Bury, Lancashire
Died
Gallipoli, Turkey 21 August 1915
Age
19
Grave or Memorial
Helles Memorial, Gallipoli, Turkey

Matthew Killoran

Bolton Journal and Guardian 10 September 1915

Corporation Workman Killed

Another Boltonian who has laid down his life for his country is **Pte. Matthew Killoran** who, while serving with the 11th Manchester Regiment in the Dardanelles, was killed in action. The gallant soldier, who resided with his wife at 3, All Saints-st., enlisted in the first week of the war at Ashton, and he had been in the fighting line about three months, being killed on the 13 August. In civil life Killoran, who was 27 years of age, was employed at the Belmont Waterworks. In his last letter home Killoran drew a copy of the Union Jack, adding the description, "the flag that knows no defeat."

Matthew was the son of Hugh Killoran b.1856, a tailor, and (Mary?) Ann Killoran b.1854.

He first appeared on the 1891 census living at 6 All Saints Street, Bolton with his parents and sister Mary Ann Killoran b.1889.

Matthew's father appears to have died shortly afterwards and his mother had another son, Henry Bibby b.1894. Matthew's mother married Charles Cuerden b.1859 as Ann Bibby in 1899.

Matthew appears (although almost illegibly) on the 1901 Census living at the same address with his mother, Charles Cuerden and his sister Mary Ann Killoran and half-brother Henry Bibby.

Matthew enlisted in the Militia as a private in the 6th Bn Manchester Regiment on 13 September 1904 and purchased his release on 21 September 1904.

He enlisted again in the Militia as a private in the 4th Bn King's Own (Royal Lancaster) Regiment on 27 October 1904 and again purchased his discharge (for £2.00) on 26 April 1905. Hiss medical examination recorded him as being 5' 2 3/8" tall, weighing 106 lbs with a fresh complexion, hazel eyes and dark brown hair. He had a tattoo of a cross on his left forearm.

He enlisted once again in the Militia as a private in the 5th Bn Manchester Regiment on 6 May 1905 at Ashton-under-Lyne - this time with grey eyes and height 5' 3 1/2". His weight was 112 lbs. "Slightly knock kneed and little toes of both feet do not touch the ground."

He enlisted for a fourth time in the Militia as a private in the 3rd Bn The Loyal North Lancashire Regiment on 7 June 1906. He deserted 2 days later and was awarded 10 days detention. His medical examination this time puzzlingly recorded his eyes as being blue. Height at that point was 5' 3 3/4" and weight 115 lbs. His cross tattoo had been joined by a letter M with two dots on the right forearm.

He enlisted yet again in the Militia as a private in the 3rd Bn King's Regiment on 23 April 1907 in Warrington. He was discharged under Para 59 Special Army Orders on 21 March 1910. Matthew's eyes reverted to being hazel on his 1907 medical examination. His height however was then just 5' and his weight was 155 lbs... His tattoo collection had grown to "Red heart pierced with arrow and feint tattoo mark outside of flags, clasped hands, True Love and dagger inside right forearm. Sword with wreath entwined inside left forearm. E.M. with scroll above and below left arm, Rose (flower) left forearm. LOVE back of left wrist." He also had a scar above his left ear, a scar behind his right ear and a linear scar on the left side of his forehead.

He appeared on the 1911 Census as an inmate of Cheetham Prison (Strangeways) in Manchester.

Matthew married Annie Cocker in Bolton in 1912. He worked as an iron turner.

Name	
	Killoran, Matthew
Rank	
	Private
Number	
	3445
Unit	
	11th Bn Manchester Regiment
Born	
	Bolton, Lancashire 1888
Enlisted	
	Ashton-Under-Lyne, Lancashire
Died	
	Gallipoli, Turkey 13 August 1915
Age	
	27
Grave or Memorial	
	Helles Memorial, Gallipoli, Turkey

William Henry Lancaster

Bolton Journal and Guardian 17 September 1915

Boltonian with Australians Killed

Mr, and Mrs. Lancaster, 4, Blackwood-St., Great Lever, have received intimation that their son **Pte. W. H. Lancaster**, was killed in the Dardanelles during the fighting from August 7th to 18th. Pte Lancaster was only 19 years of age. In Bolton he was employed at the mill of Messrs. Thomas Taylor Ltd., Saville-st. He went out to work on a farm in Australia in June last year, and enlisted in the Colonial infantry in February, being in the third battalion of the 1st Infantry Brigade. He spent a short time in Egypt, and had been in the fighting for about four months. In his letters home he spoke very cheerily, and mentioned in one that he hoped to be in Bolton for his Christmas dinner. He also wrote: "Since I arrived I have met a good many Bolton lads, so I am not without some of my old pals."

3rd Battalion Unit Diary - 7 August 1915 - Lone Pine

We held our position against continuous bombing at which the enemy appear to be very expert. Our casualties were heavy and we confidently expect from results of observation that theirs were the same. About 70 prisoners and two machine guns were captured the previous night one of which is in action against the enemy. Both our own M/guns were put out of action during the day by enemy M/gun on Johnston's Jolly. A strong counter attack was launched by the enemy on our front during the night. Bombing which has been much neglected in our training is the thing required most. Our men however demonstrated their ability to use bombs successfully and our trained men were as good as those of the enemy. The day was spent in holding our front against bombs and consolidating the line. A further 30 yards of trench was taken with this object about 1800 and prepared for defence. We had no trouble here during night 7/8th inst. Col E. S. Brown was killed and Major D. M. McConaghy assumed command.

William was the son of George Lancaster b.1857, a hawker, and Charlotte Lancaster née Ainsworth b.1847.

Charlotte been previously married to someone named Jones.

William's father had moved to the USA as a weaver. He married Charlotte in Lowell, Massachusetts, where both their children were born, but the family had returned to England in December 1899.

William appeared on the 1911 census living at 152 Blackhorse Street, Bolton with his parents and sister Alice b.1894.

Alice was employed in a bleachworks and William was a cotton weaver.

William's medical examination on enlistment recorded him as being 5' 3 7/8" tall, weighing 8 st 7 lbs with a dark complexion, brown eyes and dark hair.

Name	
Lancaster, William Henry	
Rank	
Private	
Number	
1765	
Unit	
3rd Bn Australian Imperial Force	
Born	
Lowall, Massachusetts, USA 1896	
Enlisted	
Liverpool, New South Wales, Australia 28 January 1915	
Died	
Gallipoli, Turkey August 1915	
Age	
19	
Grave or Memorial	
Lone Pine Cemetery, Gallipoli, Turkey	

William Lawrence

Bolton Journal and Guardian 30 March 1917

Killed

Reported missing on the Gallipoli Peninsula on August 9th., 1915, **Pte. WILLIAM LAWRENCE**, L.N.L. Regt., is now presumed to have died on that date. His home is at 23, Ada-st., Bolton, and he formerly worked at Messrs. Eden and Thwaites' Meetings Bleachworks. He was 20 years of age when he enlisted on September 1st, 1914, and went to Gallipoli in June, 1915. He is on the Roll of Honour at St. Matthew's Church.

William was the son of William Samuel Sebastopol Lawrence b.1856, a mechanic labourer and sometime iron driller, and Jane Lawrence née France b.1860

William first appeared on the 1901 Census living at 23 Ada Street, Bolton with his parents and siblings Louisa b.1884, Percy Stuart b.1887, Harold b.1890, Elizabeth Ann b.1892 and Alice b.1897.

The family remained unchanged at the same address in 1911 with the addition of another daughter, Ellen b.1902.

William was employed as a piecer in a cotton mill.

Name	
Greenhalgh, Harold	
Rank	
Lance Corporal	
Number	
15232	
Unit	
"A" Coy. 6th Bn The Loyal North Lancashire Regiment	
Born	
Bolton, Lancashire 1894	
Enlisted	
Bolton, Lancashire	
Died	
Gallipoli, Turkey 9 August 1915	
Age	
21	
Grave or Memorial	
Helles Memorial, Gallipoli, Turkey	

John Leach

John married Mary Jane Evans b.1885 at Emmanuel Church, Bolton in 1908.

The couple appeared on the 1911 Census living at 105 Morris Green Lane, Daubhill, Bolton with their son Robert b.1910.

John was working as an iron driller at the time.

Name	Leach, John
Rank	Private
Number	6643
Unit	1st Bn Lancashire Fusiliers
Born	Bolton, Lancashire 1881
Enlisted	Bolton, Lancashire
Died	Gallipoli, Turkey 4 June 1915
Age	34
Grave or Memorial	Helles Memorial, Gallipoli, Turkey

Roger Lindsay

Farnworth Weekly Journal 26 November 1915

KILLED ON FIRST DAY IN THE EAST

Mrs. Lindsay, 81, Peel-st., Farnworth, received word from two sources of the death of her husband, **Pte. Roger Lindsay**, of the 6th L.N.L., in the Dardanelles. The Rev. J. Clark Gibson, Wesleyan chaplain wrote as follows: - "October 31st. - By now you will have heard of the death of your husband. He only arrived last night and was hit while the enemy were shelling the lines, with a shrapnel bullet, and almost instantaneously killed. I can hardly say how deeply we were grieved, and how our sympathy goes out to you and yours in your sudden bereavement. As we laid him to rest in a little cemetery on a hill side, from which in the west can be seen the islands of the Aegean (Samothrace, Mitylene) so full of sacred memory, we were very conscious of the blessed presence of Him who speaks to us in our sorrows, saying 'Let not your hears be troubled' and 'I am the resurrection.' May you be even in your deep sorrow be comforted and strengthened by the ever present Redeemed. I have pleasant recollections of preaching in a little Wesleyan chapel at Farnworth whilst a student at Manchester, and seeing your address recalled my presence there one harvest festival."

Private Lowe of 18 Kent-st., writes to his wife:- "I am sorry to tell you that **Roger Lindsay** was killed the day we landed. He got a bullet in his chest and died in about five minutes. He did not suffer much." Pte. Albert Chapman also writes to his wife at 21. William-st. confirming the news of Pte. Lindsay's death and says, "Give Mrs. Lindsay my sympathy in her sad bereavement. Roger was one of the jolliest lads we had and we respected him very much." The deceased, who was 30 years of age, and leaves a wife and three children, enlisted on November 18th last year in the 12th L.N.L. Regiment, from which he was transferred to the 6th, and went out to the Near East some five weeks ago. He was a collier at Lord Ellesmere's Ashton Field Colliery. His wife has three brothers in the Army.

Roger was the son of Thomas Lindsay b.1857, a coal miner, and Betsy Lindsay née Brooks b.1854.

He first appeared on the 1891 Census living at 125 Darley Street, Farnworth with his parents and siblings William Thomas b.1877, Ellen b.1879, Eliza b.1882, Robert b.1884, Mary Elizabeth b.1889 and Jane b.1890.

In 1901 Roger was living at 82 Peel Street with his parents and siblings William Thomas, Ellen, Eliza, Robert, Mary Elizabeth, Jane, Lucy b.1892, Anne b.1897 and Ada b.1901. Roger was then working as a cotton dyer.

Roger married Mary Ellen Christie b.1887 at St John the Evangelist Church, Farnworth with Kearsley, Lancashire on 18 April 1908.

In 1911 the couple were living at 81 Peel Street, Farnworth with their sons, Thomas b.1909 and Walter b.1910.

Roger was working as a collier / waggoner in a coal mine.

Another son, Fred, was born in 1914.

Roger's name is on Farnworth War Memorial.

Name	Lindsay, Roger
Rank	Private
Number	11/18269
Unit	6th Bn The Loyal North Lancashire Regiment
Born	Little Lever, Lancashire 1886
Enlisted	Farnworth, Lancashire 18 November 1914
Died	Gallipoli, Turkey 31 October 1915
Age	21
Grave or Memorial	Green Hill Cemetery

Harry Lomax

Bolton Journal and Guardian 19 November 1915

A Lone Pine Hero

Mr. and Mrs. Lomax, of 4, Birmingham-st., Bolton, have received intimation of the death, about August 6th in Gallipoli, of their second son, **Private Harry Lomax**, of the 2nd Battalion, Australian Force. Deceased, who was 30 years of age, and unmarried, was educated at St. Matthew's School and the Secondary School, Bolton, and was employed for a time as a postman before emigrating to New Zealand in 1909. Later he went to Sydney, Australia, and worked at the Gas Works. He enlisted in the Australian Forces for foreign service on May 4th, and met his death in the heroic fighting at Lone Pine. His last letter was dated August 4th, and the sudden stoppage of communications led his friends to fear the worst. When in Bolton, deceased was connected with St. George's Church and Sunday School, and his brother, Robert Lomax, is in the R.A.M.C.

Harry was the son of Robert Lomax b.1851, a textile machine fitter, and Elizabeth Lomax née Smith b.1851.

Harry first appeared on the 1891 Census living at 13 Prosperous Street, Bolton with his parents and siblings James b.1879, Mary Ellen b.1881 and Bertha b.1888.

In 1901 the family were living at 4 Birmingham Street, Bolton along with 2 additional children: Bessie b.1893 and Robert b.1896.

Harry was employed as an assistant postman.

The family were still living at 4 Birmingham Street in 1911 although Harry had departed for Australia by that point.

Harry's medical examination on enlisting recorded him as being 5' 6 1/2" tall and weighing 130 lbs with a dark complexion, brown eyes and dark hair.

Name	Lomax, Harry
Rank	Private
Number	2164
Unit	2nd Bn Australian Imperial Force
Born	Bolton, Lancashire 1885
Enlisted	Liverpool, NSW, Australia 3 May 1915
Died	Gallipoli, Turkey Between 6-9 August 1915
Age	30
Grave or Memorial	Lone Pine Memorial, Gallipoli, Turkey

Joseph Lomax

Bolton Journal and Guardian 28 May 1915

Mr. and Mrs. Lomax, 22, Almond-st., Astley Bridge, have been officially informed that their son, **Lance-Corporal Joseph Lomax**, was killed in action in the Dardanelles on May 11th*. Lomax, who was in his 30th year, should have finished his time in the Army in October last. When war broke out he was in India, where he had been for the last seven years. When 13 years of age Lomax joined the Lads' Brigade belonging to St. Paul's, Astley Bridge. Afterwards he became associated with the Volunteers, and later joined the 1st Battalion Lancashire Fusiliers, and had been in the Army about nine years. Lomax, who was a first-class signaller and marksman, was well-known in the Astley Bridge district.

Joseph was the son of John Edward Lomax b.1863, a gardener and sometime self-actor minder in a cotton mill, and Mary Ellen Lomax née Simeon b.1867.

He first appeared on the 1891 Census living at 5 Lancaster Street, Bolton with his parents and sisters Mary Jane b.1889 and Elizabeth b.1890.

On the 1901 Census Joseph and his family were living at 27 Coop Street, Bolton and had gained 4 more children: Ann b.1893, Mary Ellen b.1896, William Simeon b.1898 and Margaret b.1899. Joseph was working as a piecer in a cotton mill.

Joseph enlisted in the Militia on 10 November 1903. His medical report then recorded him as being 5' 3" tall, 105 lbs with a fresh complexion, blue eyes and brown hair. He purchased his discharge (for £1) from the Army on 1 December 1903.

He enlisted again in the 4th Bn King's Own (Royal Lancaster) Regiment on 28 August 1905. By this time he had acquired a tattoo of an anchor, heart and cross on his left forearm.

By 1911 Joseph was serving in the Army in India.

The rest of the family were living at 22 Almond Street, Bolton and had been joined by two more children: Lilian b.1904 and John Edward b.1906.

* *Date of death given as 25 April on CWGC.*

Name	
Lomax, Joseph	
Rank	
Lance Corporal	
Number	
841	
Unit	
1st Bn Lancashire Fusiliers	
Born	
Bolton, Lancashire c.1885	
Enlisted	
Bury, Lancashire 28 August 1905	
Died	
Gallipoli, Turkey 25 April 1915	
Age	
29	
Grave or Memorial	
Helles Memorial, Gallipoli, Turkey	

Frank Lonsdale

Bolton Journal and Guardian 21 May 1915

Mrs. Mayoh, 158 Lorne-st., Farnworth, has received intimation from the War Office of the death of her brother, **Private T. Lonsdale*** (sic) (1616) of the 1st Battalion Lancashire Fusiliers, which occurred on May 5th form wounds received in the Dardanelles. Lonsdale, whose parents lived in the Halliwell-rd. district, Bolton, was formerly a little piecer for Messrs. Greenhalgh and Shaw, and enlisted seven years ago. Had the war not broken out he would have completed his term in the Army in August. He was then in India, where he had been for five years. His regiment was recalled, and he had three days furlough in march, which he spent with his sister. Shortly afterwards his regiment was sent to Egypt. He has since written to his brother, John W. Lonsdale, who is in the same regiment, saying he was going on all right, but the worst was yet to come. He was looking on the bright side, and believed he would get through all right. Mrs. Mayoh's husband is also serving with the 1-5th Loyal North Lancashire Regiment in France. He has seen service with the regulars in the 1st Battalion.

Frank was the son of William Lonsdale b.1843, a cotton spinner, and Hannah Lonsdale née Baldwin b.c.1845

He is listed on the 1901 Census living at 26 Weymouth Street, Bolton with his mother and siblings Elizabeth Ann b.1870, Harry (Henry?) b.1874, James b.1878, Mary (Margaret?) Ann b.1880, Robert b.1883, Hannah b.1884 and Walter b.1886.

There had been another son, John William b.1872 and a daughter, Ruth Ellen b.1874.

Frank's father William was listed as an inmate of the Bolton Union Workhouse at Townleys, Farnworth on the 1901 and 1911 Censuses.

His mother appears to have died before 1911.

In 1911 Frank was serving in India as a private soldier with the 1st Bn Lancashire Fusiliers in Multan, Punjab, India.

* F Lonsdale misprinted as T Lonsdale in Journal article.

Name	Lonsdale, Frank
Rank	Private
Number	1616
Unit	1st Bn Lancashire Fusiliers
Born	Bolton, Lancashire 1891
Enlisted	Bury, Lancashire
Died	Gallipoli, Turkey 25 April 1915
Age	25
Grave or Memorial	Helles Memorial, Gallipoli, Turkey

Name	
Lord, Albert	
Rank	
Private	
Number	
1138	
Unit	
1st/5th Bn	
Lancashire Fusiliers	
Born	
Little Lever, Lancashire	
1893	
Enlisted	
Bury, Lancashire	
Died	
Gallipoli, Turkey	
26 July 1915	
Age	
20	
Grave or Memorial	
Helles Memorial	
Gallipoli, Turkey	

Albert Lord

Albert was the son of Alfred Lord b.1871, a coal miner hewer, and Ann Lord née Bradley b.1872.

In 1901 Alfred was living at 6 High Street, Little Lever with his parents and brother Fred b.1896.

His older brother William Henry b.1891 was living with his grandparents in Little Lever at the time of the Census.

In 1911 he was living at 19 Waverley Place, Radcliffe, Lancashire with his father and brothers. His mother was not present although his father was listed as being married rather than widowed.

Alfred was working as a warp dyer.

Henry Lowe

Bolton Journal and Guardian 17 December 1915

Bradshaw Farmer's Son Killed in Gallipoli

A communication from the War Office has been received by Mr. and Mrs. Andrew Lowe, Bradshaw Head Farm, Bradshaw, announcing the death of their son, **Private Harry Lowe**, 1st Battalion, Essex Regiment, Which occurred in Gallipoli on November 15th. Deceased enlisted in January in the R.F.A., and after a period of training at Newcastle, proceeded to Essex, where he was transferred to the Essex Regiment, and sailed from England to the Eastern theatre of war at the beginning of September. Before enlisting Lowe assisted his father on the farm, and went daily rounds with in Bolton with the milk float. He was 19 years of age and his name appears on the Roll of Honour at St. Mary's Church Schools, Hawkshaw-lane, which he attended. A message of sympathy has been forwarded to the parents by the headmaster, Mr. T. Beckett. Deceased and the late Private Victor Green, of Higher Barn Farm, Harwood, who was killed in Gallipoli on October 5th, were chums and both enlisted at the same time.

Henry was the son of Andrew Lowe b.1859, a dairy farmer, and Abigail Lowe née Pendlebury b.1863.

Henry first appeared on the 1901 Census living at Bradshaw Head Farm with his parents and his siblings John b.1883, Thomas b.1884, Anne b.1892, James b.1894, Alice b.1899 and Alfred b.1900.

The family group remained much the same at the farm in 1911 except that John was no longer present and there were two more sons, Stanley b.1904 and Fred b.1908.

Of the 12 children 3 had died by 1911.

Henry was employed as a plaiter down in a calico mill.

Name	Lowe, Henry
Rank	Private
Number	20181
Unit	1st Bn Essex Regiment
Born	Harwood, Lancashire 1896
Enlisted	Bolton, Lancashire
Died	Gallipoli, Turkey 15 November 1915
Age	19
Grave or Memorial	Azmak Cemetery, Suvla, Gallipoli, Turkey

Name	
Lowe, John	
Rank	
Corporal	
Number	
1997	
Unit	
1st/5th Bn Manchester Regiment	
Born	
Warrington, Lancashire 1880	
Enlisted	
Wigan, Lancashire	
Died	
Gallipoli, Turkey 18 May 1915	
Age	
35	
Grave or Memorial	
Helles Memorial, Gallipoli, Turkey	

John Lowe

John was the son of Thomas Lowe b.1836, a watchman and sometime smith, and Ellen Lowe née Caldwell b.1841.

In 1881 John was living at 42 Napier Street, Warrington with his parents and siblings Mary Ann b.1862, Robert b.1866, William b.1871, Gilbert b.1873, Joseph b.1875 and James Robey b.1877.

In 1891 John was a boarding pupil at the Blue Coat School, Warrington.

In 1901 John was living at 16 Atherton Road, Hindley, Lancashire with his uncle Joseph Houghton and aunt Eliza Houghton née Lowe. He was working as a house painter, which was also his uncle's profession.

John married Clara Hetty Gregory at St Bartholomew's Church, Westhoughton on 13 April 1903.

In 1911 the couple were living at 770 Wigan Road, Westhoughton with their son Roger b.1908.

John was still working as a house painter.

They had two other children - Frederick b.1912 and Olive b.1914.

His name is on Westhoughton War Memorial.

George Lyons

George's name appears on the Bolton Borough Roll of Honour.

Name	Lyons, George
Rank	Private
Number	6280
Unit	1st Bn Lancashire Fusiliers
Born	
Enlisted	
Died	Gallipoli, Turkey 4 June 1915
Age	
Grave or Memorial	Helles Memorial, Gallipoli, Turkey

Name
Macdonald, Jonah Boyd

Rank
Private

Number
17652

Unit
6th Bn
The Loyal North
Lancashire Regiment

Born
Bolton, Lancashire
1890

Enlisted
Bolton, Lancashire

Died
Gallipoli, Turkey
9 August 1915

Age
25

Grave or Memorial
Helles Memorial,
Gallipoli, Turkey

Jonah Boyd Macdonald

Jonah was the son of Alexander Macdonald b.1857, a tool fitter, and Berthina Macdonald b.1858.

He first appeared on the 1901 Census living at 1 Frederick Street, Bolton with his parents and siblings Berthina b.1879, Jeannie b.1881, Eleanor b.1883, Elizabeth b.1885, Alexander b.1888, Jessie b.1895.

In 1911 the family were living at 29 John Street, Bolton.

Alexander was no longer present - or noticed - as the Census reported only six children having been born and none having died!

Jonah was employed as a side piecer in a cotton mill in 1911.

Henry Marsden

Bolton Journal and Guardian 10 December 1915

Killed in Gallipoli

Mr. M. Marsden, 96, Darley-st., has received word from the War Office that his third son, **Pte. H. Marsden** has been killed in action. The casualty is given in an Alexandria list. Pte. Marsden, who was in the 1st Lancashire Fusiliers, was 26 years of age, and unmarried. He had been in the Army seven years, six of which were spent in India, where he was stationed when the war commenced. He had five days leave in January, after which he proceeded to the Dardanelles. He was slightly wounded on April 25th, and rejoined his unit on May 26th. Prior to enlisting he was a moulder at Messrs. Dobson and Barlow's. As a boy he attended the Draycott-st. School. His eldest brother, James, who was in the same battalion, died from wounds during April.

Henry (Harry) was the son of Malachi Marsden b.1856, a stripper grinder in a cotton mill, and Alice Marsden née Ramsbottom b.1858.

He first appeared on the 1891 Census living at 25 Boardman Street, Bolton with his parents and siblings, Mary Jane Ramsbottom (not Marsden) b.1877, Ellen b.1879, Lily b.1880, James b.1883, Annie b.1885, David b.1886 and Susannah b.1888.

By 1901 he was living with his parents at 1 Raby Street, Bolton with his parents and siblings Ellen, Lily, James, Annie, David, Susannah, Esther b.1892, William b.1894, Norman b.1897 and Florrie b.1899.

He enlisted in the Militia as a private in the 6th Bn Lancashire Fusiliers in 1906.

His medical examination recorded him as being 5' 6 1/2" tall, weighing 111 lbs with a fresh complexion, blue eyes and red hair.

In 1911 Henry was serving in the 1st Bn Lancashire Fusiliers in India.

Name	
Marsden, Harry	
Rank	
Private	
Number	
1295	
Unit	
1st Bn Lancashire Fusiliers	
Born	
Bolton, Lancashire c.1889	
Enlisted	
Bury, Lancashire 3 October 1906	
Died	
Gallipoli, Turkey 4 June 1915	
Age	
26	
Grave or Memorial	
Helles Memorial, Gallipoli, Turkey	

Name
Marsden, James
Rank
Private
Number
13516
Unit
1st Bn
Lancashire Fusiliers
Born
Bolton, Lancashire
1883
Enlisted
Bury, Lancashire
Died
Gallipoli, Turkey
14 June 1915
Age
33
Grave or Memorial
Pieta Military Cemetery, Malta

James Marsden

Bolton Journal and Guardian 10 December 1915

Killed in Gallipoli

Mr. M. Marsden, 96, Darley-st., has received word from the War Office that his third son, **Pte. H. Marsden** has been killed in action. The casualty is given in an Alexandria list. Pte. Marsden, who was in the 1st Lancashire Fusiliers, was 26 years of age, and unmarried. He had been in the Army seven years, six of which were spent in India, where he was stationed when the war commenced. He had five days leave in January, after which he proceeded to the Dardanelles. He was slightly wounded on April 25th, and rejoined his unit on May 26th. Prior to enlisting he was a moulder at Messrs. Dobson and Barlow's. As a boy he attended the Draycott-st. School. His eldest brother, James, who was in the same battalion, died from wounds during April*.

James was the son of Malachi Marsden b.1856, a stripper grinder in a cotton mill, and Alice Marsden née Ramsbottom b.1858.

He first appeared on the 1891 Census living at 25 Boardman Street, Bolton with his parents and siblings, Mary Jane Ramsbottom (not Marsden) b.1877, Ellen b.1879, Lily b.1880, Annie b.1885, David b.1886, Susannah b.1888 and Henry b.1889.

By 1901 he was living with his parents at 1 Raby Street, Bolton with his parents and siblings Ellen, Lily, Annie, David, Susannah, Henry, Esther b.1892, William b.1894, Norman b.1897 and Florrie b.1899.

He married Louisa Webster b.1884 at Higher Bridge Street Primitive Methodist Church, Bolton, Lancashire on 27 February 1904.

They appeared on the 1911 Census living at 13 Raby Street with their 3 children, Malachi b.1907, James b.1909 and Elsie b.1910.

James was employed as a belt repairer at an iron foundry in 1911.

* Actual date of death was 14 June 1915.

Thomas Marsden

Bolton Journal and Guardian 8 October 1915

Deane Soldier Missing

A goodly number of Boltonians have been posted as missing in the operations in the Gallipoli Peninsula, and the list is augmented by the inclusion of the name of **Pte. Thos. Marsden**, 1st battalion Border Regiment, the son of Mr. W. Marsden, 4, Gordon-avenue, Deane. The gallant soldier took part in the fighting on August 21st but since then nothing has been heard of him. He enlisted in November last in the 3rd Battalion, and was stationed for some time at Carlisle and Shoeburyness, but learning that the 1st Battalion were under orders to proceed to the front, and being very eager to get on active service he applied for and received his transfer. He landed at the Dardanelles on may 8th, and received his baptism of fire a few hours afterwards. Since then he has been in several important engagements, but until August 21st he escaped unscathed. Pte. Marsden, who was only 19 years of age, worked in civil life at Tong's Brewery, and was on the Roll of Honour at The Saviour's Church.

Thomas was the son of William Marsden b.1876, a petrol motor waggon driver, and Maria Marsden née Caterall b.1877.

He first appeared on the 1901 Census living in Liverpool Road, Penwortham, Lancashire with his parents and sisters Eva b.1886 and Ada Alice b.1901.

By 1911 Thomas and his parents had moved to 17 Bankfield Street, Bolton with children Eva, Ada Alice, James b.1904 and Victor William b.1908.

Thomas was then employed as a little piecer in a textile spinning mill.

His parents later lived at the Antelope Hotel, Little Hulton.

Name
Marsden, Thomas
Rank
Private
Number
18134
Unit
1st Bn Border Regiment
Born
Leyland, Lancashire c.1896
Enlisted
Bolton, Lancashire November 1914
Died
Gallipoli, Turkey 21 August 1915
Age
19
Grave or Memorial
Helles Memorial, Gallipoli, Turkey

John Robert Martland

Bolton Journal and Guardian 17 September 1915

More 6th Lancashire Losses After Suvla Bay Landing

Reports continue to come to hand of local casualties in the 6th Batt. Loyal North Lancashire Regiment, on the Gallipoli Peninsula. **Pte. J. R. Martland**, whose wife resides at 117, Mill Hill-st., has been missing since August 9th. He was one of the early volunteers for imperial service, enlisting during the early days of the war. After training in various centres in England he sailed with his battalion to join the Mediterranean Expeditionary Force and in a letter written by him on the 3rd August he described the severe character of the fighting and the work the battalion had done in the trenches. Prior to the war, Pte. Martland, who is 26 years of age, was employed at Messrs. Blair and Sumner's, Mill Hill Bleachworks.

Bolton Journal and Guardian 1 December 1916

An official report received by Mrs. Martland, 117, Mill Hill-st., Bolton, states that her husband, **Pte. JOHN R. MARTLAND**, Loyal North Lancashire Regiment, is now included amongst those presumed to have died. He had been missing since an engagement in Gallipoli on August 9th, 1915, nearly 12 months after joining the Colours. Twenty-six years of age, and an old boy of St. John's School, Martland formerly worked at Messrs. Blair and Sumner's Bleachworks, Mill Hill. He leaves two children.

John was the son of James Martland b.1868, a cloth drier at a bleachworks, and Catherine Martland née Tankard b.1868.

He first appeared (listed as Markland) on the 1891 Census living at 38 Craddock Street, Bolton with his parents, great-grandmother, aunt and sister Edith b.1890.

On the 1901 Census (again listed as Markland) he was living at 5 Hope Street with his parents and siblings Edith, Mary Alice b.1893, Annie b.1896, James Nathan b.1899.

By 1911 the family (finally listed as Martland!) were living at 5 Kestor Street, Bolton and had had another son, Fred b.1906.

John was employed as a bleacher's labourer.

John married Mary Alice Marsh at St John's Church, Bolton in 1913.

Name	
Martland, John Robert	
Rank	
Private	
Number	
11537	
Unit	
6th Bn The Loyal North Lancashire Regiment	
Born	
Bolton, Lancashire 1889	
Enlisted	
Bolton, Lancashire 1914	
Died	
Gallipoli, Turkey 9 August 1915	
Age	
26	
Grave or Memorial	
Helles Memorial, Gallipoli, Turkey	

James Mather

Bolton Journal and Guardian 10 September 1915

Boltonians in Fierce Engagement

NORTH LANCASHIRE MEN MISSING IN GALLIPOLI

The 6th Battalion of the Loyal North Lancashire Regiment suffered in Gallipoli in an engagement on August 9th. A number of Bolton soldiers are in this Battalion, and one, **Private James Mather** (12151), of A Company, is announced as missing. Private Mather resided with his parents at 62, Sloane-st., Daubhill. Prior to the outbreak of war, he was employed at the Hulton Colliery. He enlisted on August 27th, and after having been in training in Preston, Tidworth, Winchester, and Blackdown, left England in the middle of June.

James was the son of William Henry Mather b.1871, a coal miner hewer, and Alice Mather née McDona b.1871.

James first appeared on the 1901 Census living at 15 Smethurst Lane, Bolton with his parents, aunt and siblings Lily M b.1894, George b.1898 and Thomas Henry b.1901.

By 1911 he was living at 62 Sloane Street, Bolton with his parents and siblings George b., Thomas Henry, Helena b1905. and Edith b.1908.

James was employed as a piecer in a cotton spinning mill.

Name	Mather, James
Rank	Private
Number	12151
Unit	6th Bn The Loyal North Lancashire Regiment
Born	Bolton, Lancashire c.1896
Enlisted	Bolton, Lancashire
Died	Gallipoli, Turkey 9 August 1915
Age	19
Grave or Memorial	Helles Memorial, Gallipoli, Turkey

Bolton Journal and Guardian 24 December 1915

Quartermaster's Fine Record

By the death of **Company-Quartermaster Sergt. Hugh McCarthy** (3504), 6th L.N.L., whose wife, residing at 16, Claughton-st., is officially informed that he died on November 24th from wounds received with the Mediterranean Forces, light is thrown on a splendid record of service. An old soldier, McCarthy was one of the heroic defenders of Ladysmith in the South African War, losing the first finger of his right hand in the famous siege, and though his career has ended in Gallipoli, he was one of Sir John French's first army who checked the German advance on Calais many months ago. Joining the Army at 17, he was with the King's Liverpool Regiment in the African campaign, and completing nine years went on pension. He was employed at Lee's Victory Ironworks when the present war began, and still in his prime - he was only 36 - re-enlisted in the L.N.L. on August 29th last year, and within five weeks was in the thick of the fighting in France. McCarthy took part in severe engagements at Ypres and La Bassee, and at the former place was wounded in the right arm. He arrived in Manchester on Christmas Eve and after six weeks in hospital at Ashton-under-Lyme, enjoyed a month at home before joining a unit at Felixstowe. His services were highly valued as an old campaigner, and, drafted to the Mediterranean, he rose from the rank of corporal to company-quartermaster sergeant. He wrote home five days before the date of his death, and made no mention of anything amiss. Mrs. McCarthy is left with five young children, the eldest aged eight. Deceased was an adherent of SS Peter and Paul's Church and appears on the Roll of Honour there.

Hugh was the son of John McCarthy b.1843, an iron puddler, and Mary Ann McCarthy née Broderick b.1845.

In 1881 Hugh was living at 2 Back Rothwell Street, Bolton with his parents, uncle and siblings Sarah A b.1869, Denis b.1871, Mary E b.1873 and Catherine b.1881.

In 1891 Hugh, Denis and Mary were living at 4 Barn Street, Bolton with their aunts, Margaret and Ann Broderick.

Hugh enlisted in the Militia with the King's Liverpool Regiment at Warrington on 1 October 1896. At the time he was employed as a moulder for Bolton Engineering Company. His medical examination recorded him as being 5' 5 1/2" tall with a florid complexion, blue eyes and dark brown hair.

On 17 November 1896 he enlisted in the King's Liverpool Regiment as a regular soldier. He was eventually promoted to Corporal for a short period but was reduced to the ranks late in 1899 after a disciplinary offence and completed his full service in November 1908 as a private soldier.

He served in South Africa from 1899 to 1902.

Hugh married Mary Ann Harkin b.1878 at Ss Peter and Paul's RC Church, Bolton 18 August 1906.

In 1911 they were living at 13 Baldwin Street, Bolton with their children Ellen b.1908 and Gerard b.1910. Hugh was then working as a hoop iron roller.

The couple had 3 more children - Agnes b.1911, Alice b.1913 and Kathleen b.1915.

After re-enlisting at the start of the war in 1914 Hugh was rapidly promoted from private to Sergeant. He became Company Quartermaster Sergeant in the field at Gallipoli.

His final field promotion to Company Sergeant Major was confirmed posthumously.

Name
McCarthy, Hugh
Rank
Company Sergeant Major
Number
3504
Unit
6th Bn The Loyal North Lancashire Regiment
Born
Bolton, Lancashire c.1878
Enlisted
Bolton, Lancashire 29 August 1914
Died
Gallipoli, Turkey 24 November 1915
Age
37
Grave or Memorial
Hill 10 Cemetery, Gallipoli, Turkey

Martin McDermott

Bolton Journal and Guardian 17 December 1915

Killed in Gallipoli

Pte. Martin McDermott (4250), whose wife and three children reside at 31, Acton-st., Halliwell, served in the South African war, and was wounded at Spion Kop. When the present war broke out he re-offered his services and left for the Dardanelles with the 1st Lancashire Fusiliers on June 2nd. He was reported missing on June 4th, and nothing further was heard of him until recently, when he was officially stated to have been killed in action. McDermott, who was 34 years of age, entered the army as a boy, and when the South African war ended he had completed nine years. He was employed by Messrs. Dickinson's, St. George's-rd., as a labourer. His four brothers are serving the colours.

Martin was the son of Patrick McDermott b.1844, a general labourer, and Bridget McDermott b.1848.

He appears on the 1891 Census living at 27 Back Crook Street with his parents and siblings, Mary Ellen b.1872, Maggie b.1874, Peter b.1876, Patrick b.1878, Annie b.1879 and Bernard b.1883.

Martin Married Elizabeth Ann Armstrong b.1886 at St Mary's Church, Bolton on 7 October 1905.

In 1911 they were living at 30 Acton Street, Bolton with their sons John Henry b.1906 and Thomas b.1908.

At that time Martin was employed as a labourer in bleachworks - he also gives his place of birth as being Bolton.

Elizabeth remarried to John W Ackers in Bolton in 1918.

Name
McDermott, Martin
Rank
Private
Number
4250
Unit
1st Bn Lancashire Fusiliers
Born
Rotherham, Yorkshire c.1881
Enlisted
Bury, Lancashire
Died
Gallipoli, Turkey 4 June 1915
Age
34
Grave or Memorial
Helles Memorial, Gallipoli, Turkey

Name	
	McDowell, Alexander James
Rank	
	Private
Number	
	15654
Unit	
	6th Bn The Loyal North Lancashire Regiment
Born	
	Bolton, Lancashire 1896
Enlisted	
	Bolton, Lancashire September 1914
Died	
	Gallipoli, Turkey 12 August 1915
Age	
	19
Grave or Memorial	
	Helles Memorial, Gallipoli, Turkey

Alexander James McDowell

Bolton Journal and Guardian 10 September 1915

Boltonians in Fierce Engagement

NORTH LANCASHIRE MEN MISSING IN GALLIPOLI

Information has been received that **Pte. Alex. James McDowell**, (19), one of the sons of W. W. McDowell, 200, Escrick-st., who has given three sons to the services, died of wounds on August 12th. The gallant soldier, who enlisted during the rush to the recruiting office a year ago a week ago this week, was attached to the L.N.L. Regiment, with which he went to Gallipoli in June last year. Prior to leaving England he had been training at Preston, Winchester, Tidworth and Blackdown. In civil life he was engaged by Mr. Percy Southern, Blackburn-rd, Garage. He was also an enthusiastic member of St. Joseph's Confraternity.

Alexander was the son of Walter William McDowell b.1862, a baker and corn and flour dealer, and Mary Ann McDowell née Pape b.1864.

He first appeared on the 1901 Census living at 345 Halliwell Road, Bolton with his parents and siblings Elizabeth b.1887, Helen (Ellen) b.1888, Annie b.1890, William b.1893, John Henry b.1894, Gertrude Westby b.1898 and Florence b.1900.

By 1911 the family were living at 200 Eskrick Street, Bolton with additional children Herbert b.1901, Hannah Moss b.1904 and Charles Edward b.1900.

Alexander was employed as a cop packer in a cotton mill.

Joseph McKenna

Bolton Journal and Guardian 8 October 1915

TWO OF FOUR SOLDIER BROTHERS KILLED

Sergt. John McKenna, 3rd Battalion Loyal North Lancashire Regiment, whose wife lives at 117, Moncrieffe-st., is one of four soldier brothers, two of whom have laid down their lives for their country. **Sergt.-Major Joe McKenna** was killed in the Dardanelles on Sept. 9th. He was in the 9th Battalion Lancashire Fusiliers, and had served 21 years in the Army before the outbreak of war, when he re-enlisted. Private Morris McKenna lost his life at the front in France whilst serving with the 2nd Manchester Regiment. He was called up at the commencement of the war, being on the reserve. Sergt.-Major John McKenna is at present at Felixstowe, having been invalided home after seven months in the trenches in France and Flanders, whilst Neil, whose time in the Army had expired, re-enlisted, and is now fighting in the Dardanelles.

Joseph was the son of John P McKenna b.c.1849, a joiner and labourer, and Ann McKenna b.c.1843.

He appeared on the 1891 Census living at 114 Spring Gardens with his parents and siblings Neil b.1876, John b.1878, Ambrose b.1880 and Ann b.1884.

Joseph was working as a cotton piecer at the time.

Name	
McKenna, Joseph	
Rank	
Company Sergeant Major	
Number	
4559	
Unit	
9th Bn Lancashire Fusiliers	
Born	
Bolton, Lancashire 1874	
Enlisted	
Bury, Lancashire	
Died	
Gallipoli, Turkey 7 August 1915	
Age	
41	
Grave or Memorial	
Helles Memorial, Gallipoli, Turkey	

John McLoughlin

Bolton Journal and Guardian 2 July 1915

A Hero of the Dardanelles

The War Office have notified Mrs. Thomasson, 24 Ralph-st., Bolton, that her cousin, **Pte. J. McLoughlin**, of the 1st Lancashire Fusiliers, has been killed in action in the Dardanelles. McLoughlin, who was 30 years of age, enlisted about six years ago in the 1st Lancashire Fusiliers, and they went to Ireland. They were afterwards drafted to India and there he has served the greater portion of his time. His regiment came to England in January, and were billeted at Nuneaton. After a few days furlough he departed for the front on March 17th. In his last letter he says they are "in the thick of it, and it will not be long before the war is over as we are about to make the great effort which will be the turning point of the war."

John was the son of James McLoughlin b.1857, a labourer, and Sarah McLoughlan née Grimes b.1852.

He first appeared on the 1891 Census living at 47 Lees Street, Bolton with his parents and brothers James b.1880, Thomas b.1882 and William b.1890.

In 1901 - at the age of 14 - he was lodging at 41 Tyndall Street, Bolton in the household of George and Selina Denton.

Name	McLoughlin, John
Rank	Private
Number	1691
Unit	1st Bn Lancashire Fusiliers
Born	Bolton Lancashire c.1885
Enlisted	Bury, Lancashire
Died	Gallipoli, Turkey 9 May 1915
Age	30
Grave or Memorial	Helles Memorial, Gallipoli, Turkey

George Edwin Melling

Farnworth Weekly Journal 16 July 1915

KILLED IN THE DARDANELLES

Mr. Melling. licensee of the Bull's Head hotel, Farnworth, has been informed that his son, **Pte. George Melling**, of the Lancashire Fusiliers was killed in action on June 2nd. He was 27 years of age and has been in the Army six years, and most of his training has been in India. After returning from India he came home for a short furlough and then went with his regiment to the Dardanelles. His parents have received no tidings from him since April, and then they only got a post card. He formerly attended the Queen-street Seminary Day School, and was concerned with the Queen-st Primitive Methodist Church and whilst in the Army kept up his association with the men's class. Soon after Christmas he came home on furlough and attended the school to personally thank the officers, teachers and scholars for their Christmas gifts. He was possessed of a fair tenor voice and favoured several P.S.A.s with solos.

George was the son of Albert Melling b.1866, landlord of the Bull's Head, Farnworth and previously a cotton spinner, and Mary Melling née Hindley b.1861.

In 1891 George was living at 12 Anvil Street, Farnworth with his parents.

He appeared on the 1901 Census living at 32 Wellington Street, Farnworth with his parents and siblings Bertha Jane b.1892 and William b.1894.

On the 1911 Census George was listed as a private soldier with 1st Bn Lancashire Fusiliers in their barracks at South Tidworth, Hampshire.

By then his parents and siblings were living at 6 Bent Street, Kearsley.

George's name is on Farnworth War Memorial.

Name	Melling, George Edwin
Rank	Private
Number	1868
Unit	1st Bn Lancashire Fusiliers
Born	Farnworth, Lancashire 1888
Enlisted	Bury, Lancashire
Died	Gallipoli, Turkey 2 June 1915
Age	27
Grave or Memorial	Helles Memorial, Gallipoli, Turkey

John Miller

Bolton Journal and Guardian 15 October 1915

A Youthful Patriot's Death

Though he was killed so long ago as the 21st August information has only just been received by his mother, Mrs. Miller, 221, Spa-rd., of the death of her son, **Private John Miller**. The dead hero, who was only 18 years of age, had been a year in the Imperial services, having been so very keen to volunteer that he enrolled in the Lancashire Fusiliers when he was only 17. He went out with his battalion to the Dardanelles about the middle of July, and had been fighting in Gallipoli Peninsula about a month before he met his death. Prior to the war Miller was in the employ of Messrs. Magee, Marshall and Co. A brother, Thomas, is a sergeant in the Royal Field Artillery. He was in the Expeditionary Force and took part in the retreat from Mons. When in France he was run over by a gun carriage, and for a time after his recovery he was on instruction duty in London, but he is now in the fighting line.

John was the son of John Miller b.1863, a brewery worker, and Ellen Miller née Hilton b.1863.

John first appeared on the 1901 Census living at 81 Belle Green Lane Ince-in-Makerfield, Lancashire with his parents and siblings Margaret b.1885, Mary b.1889, Alice b.1891, Thomas b.1892 and Nellie b.1894.

By 1911 he John was living at 130 Willows Lane, Bolton with his parents and sisters Mary, Alice and Nellie.

He was working at that time as a little piecer in a cotton spinning mill.

Name	Miller, John
Rank	Private
Number	3804
Unit	1st Bn Lancashire Fusiliers
Born	Ince-in-Makerfield, Lancashire c.1897
Enlisted	Bury, Lancashire
Died	Gallipoli, Turkey 21 August 1915
Age	18
Grave or Memorial	Helles Memorial, Gallipoli, Turkey

James Morris

Bolton Journal and Guardian

Dardanelles Hero Dies From Wounds

Mrs. J. Morris 3, Little-st., Bolton, has received word that her husband, Pte. **James Morris** (18544), 6th Battalion, L.N.L. Regt., has died from wounds received in the Dardanelles. Pte. Morris was wounded on November 13th, and was transferred to hospital at Malta, where he died on December 12th. He enlisted on December 1st, 1914, and received his training at Felixstowe prior to being drafted to the Dardanelles on August 28th. Before he enlisted he was employed at Messrs. H. Bessemer and Co., Ltd., Blackhorse-st. He was on the Roll of Honour at St. Patrick's, and was 34 years of age. He leaves a wife and five children. Two brothers of Morris are in the Army. One, Pte. John Morris, is in hospital suffering from wounds received in the Dardanelles, whilst the other, Pte. William Morris, is with the East Lancashire regiment in France.

Name	Morris, James
Rank	Private
Number	18544
Unit	6th Bn The Loyal North Lancashire Regiment
Born	Bolton, Lancashire 1881
Enlisted	Bolton, Lancashire 1 December 1914
Died	Gallipoli, Turkey 12 December 1915
Age	34
Grave or Memorial	Addolorata Cemetery, Malta

Name	
Morris, William	
Rank	
Private	
Number	
5921	
Unit	
1st Bn	
Lancashire Fusiliers	
Born	
Hull, Yorkshire	
c.1876	
Enlisted	
Horwich, Lancashire	
Died	
Gallipoli, Turkey	
9 May 1915	
Age	
39	
Grave or Memorial	
Helles Memorial,	
Gallipoli, Turkey	

William Morris

William was the son of Jonathan Morris b.1845, a labourer on a water pipe track, and Hannah Maria Morris b.1844.

He appeared on the 1891 Census living at 25 Dale Street West, Horwich with his parents and 5 assorted lodgers.

William married Emily Wright b.1883 at Holy Trinity Church, Horwich in 1904.

In 1911 the couple were living at 16 Julia Street, Horwich with their children Jonathan b.1905, Mary b.1906 and Anne b.1910.

William was employed as a kiln setter at the time.

Abraham Moscrop

Abraham's name appears on the Bolton Borough Roll of Honour.

Name	Moscrop, Abraham
Rank	Private
Number	2180
Unit	1st Bn Lancashire Fusiliers
Born	
Enlisted	
Died	Gallipoli, Turkey 30 April 1915
Age	
Grave or Memorial	Helles Memorial, Gallipoli, Turkey

Edward Mullaney

Bolton Journal and Guardian 24 September 1916

Missing in Gallipoli

Word has been received from the War Office by his mother at 9, Antelope Court, Churchgate, that **Lce-Corporal Ed. Mullaney** (16,366) Royal Irish Fusiliers, has been missing since an engagement in Gallipoli on Aug. 7th. Lance-Corporal Mullaney was 30 years of age. He had served for two years in the militia before enlisting in August last year. He underwent training at Dublin, and left Ireland for the Dardanelles about three months ago. Prior to enlisting he was employed in a dyeworks at Middleton.

Edward was the son of James Mullaney b.1855, a lodging house keeper and Dorothy Mullaney née b.1856.

In 1881 James and Dorothy ran a lodging house at 22 Blackhorse Street, Bolton. They had 3 children, John James b.1874, Ellen b.1877 and Catherine b.1879.

James died in 1889.

Edward first appeared on the 1891 Census living at 3 Back Bristol Street, Bolton with his mother and siblings Ellen, Margaret (Maggie) b.1882 and William b.1889.

John James was absent from the household.

In 1901 Edward was living with the reappeared John James (now head of the family), his mother and siblings Margaret and William.

By 1911 Edward had moved to 19 Wellington Street, Chadderton with head of household James (who had dropped his first name by that point), his mother and younger brother William.

Edward was then employed as a labourer in a cotton finishing and print works.

Name
Mullaney, Edward
Rank
Lance Corporal
Number
16366
Unit
6th Bn Royal Irish Fusiliers
Born
Bolton, Lancashire c.1885
Enlisted
Oldham, Lancashire August 1914
Died
Gallipoli, Turkey 9 August 1915
Age
30
Grave or Memorial
Helles Memorial, Gallipoli, Turkey

George Alfred Naylor

Bolton Journal and Guardian 10 September 1915

Lost with the Royal Edward

Several Boltonians were on board the Royal Edward when she was torpedoed and sunk in the Mediterranean on the 13th August, and Mr. William Naylor, 79. Venture-st., has received information that his son, **Private George A. Naylor**, Border Regiment, was not seen after the disaster, and that it is feared he was drowned. On the out ward passage Private Naylor sent a note from Malta, and that was the last communication received from him. He enlisted at the Town Hall shortly after the beginning of the present year, and, having undergone his training at Southend, he was drafted to Gallipoli. Before he attached himself to the Army, Private Naylor, who was 27 years of age, and was on the roll of honour at Slaterfield Wesleyan Church, was a spinner, being employed at Messrs. Marsden's No. 2 Albion Mills

George was the only child of William Naylor b.1863, an operative cotton spinner / minder, and Margaret Naylor née Stredder b.1864.

George first appeared (as George E Naylor) on the 1891 Census living at 27 Platt Street, Bolton with his parents.

By 1901 the family had moved to 41 Platt Street, Bolton.

In 1911 they were living at 83 Platt Street with two lodgers.

George was then employed as a piecer in a cotton mill.

By the time of his enlistment George was living at 79 Venture Street, Bolton and was working as a minder in a cotton mill.

He lost his life alongside hundreds of others when HMT Royal Edward was torpedoed by the German submarine UB-14 while en route from Alexandria to Lemnos. The ship was carrying 1367 officers and men destined for Gallipoli.

Name	Naylor, George Alfred
Rank	Private
Number	1921
Unit	1st Bn Border Regiment
Born	Bolton, Lancashire 4 September 1888
Enlisted	Bolton, Lancashire 11 January 1915
Died	At sea 13 August 1915
Age	27
Grave or Memorial	Helles Memorial, Gallipoli, Turkey

Henry Newell

Bolton Journal and Guardian 13 August 1915

Died from Enteric in Egypt

News has been received from his mother, on his 21st birthday, of the death on July, 27th, in Egypt, through enteric fever*, of **Corpl. H. Newell**, 75, Rishton-lane, Great Lever, 1st Field Ambulance, East Lancashire Division. Newell had served for four years, and was called up at the commencement of the war, and was eventually drafted to the Dardanelles. He was employed at the L. and N. W. Goods Office, and was highly esteemed by all his workmates. He was connected with All Souls' Church.

Henry was the son of Joseph Burn Newell b.1864, an insurance inspector, and Rebecca Newell née Walmsley b.1866.

Henry first appeared on the 1901 Census living at 5 York Street, Wigan with his parents and brother Ernest Edward b.1890.

Joseph Burn Newell appears on the 1911 Census living in Bargoed, Glamorganshire, managing a laundry and (apparently) married to a different woman, Anne and with another son Clifford b.1905.

Rebecca appears on the 1911 Census working as a servant for Ellis and Betsy Pollitt at 332 St Helens Road, Bolton. She is listed as being married but having no children.

Henry is listed on the 1911 Census as lodging at 7 Peace Street, Bolton in the household of John and Isabella Orrell. He was employed as a railway time keeper.

His father had worked on the railways as a young man.

Henry's medical examination on enlisting in the Army recorded his height as 5' 9 1/2".

On Henry's military record his mother was recorded as having remarried as Smith. His father was recorded as 'None'.

Henry's brother Ernest Edward Newell emigrated to Australia and served with the Australian Imperial Force at Gallipoli and later in France. He was wounded in action there but survived the war and lived to the age of 81.

Ernest's military records show that his mother Rebecca had moved to the Isle of Man by 1917.

* Typhoid

Name	Henry Newll
Rank	Corporal
Number	114
Unit	1st East Lancashire Field Ambulance, Royal Army Medical Corps
Born	Preston, Lancashire 4 Aug 1894
Enlisted	Bolton, Lancashire 7 April 1911
Died	Port Said, Egypt 27 July 1915
Age	20
Grave or Memorial	Port Said War Memorial Cemetery, Port Said, Egypt

William Henry Nield

Bolton Journal and Guardian 15 October 1915

Westhoughton Soldier Killed in Gallipoli

The 1st Battalion Lancashire Fusiliers have met with heavy losses in Gallipoli, and the latest local soldier to be reported killed is Pte. (13622) **Wm. Henry Nield**, 667, Manchester-rd., Chequerbent. Nield, who lived with his parents prior to enlisting met his death on September 6th. He was 18 years of age and was employed at the Pretoria Pit. He was a member of the Chequerbent Church Bible Class and was much respected in the district in which he resided. He enlisted in January and had been in the trenches about a month.

William was the son of Henry Nield b.1862, a coal miner, and Betty Nield née b.1859.

William first appeared on the 1901 Census living at 344 Ringley Road, Outwood with his parents and siblings John Arthur b.1884, Jonathon b.18868, Alice b.1888 and Robert b.1890.

In 1911 William was living at 667 Manchester Road, Chequerbent, Westhoughton with his parents and siblings Robert and Mary Elizabeth b.1893.

William was then employed as a nut and screw maker.

His name is on Westhoughton War Memorial.

Name	
Nield, William Henry	
Rank	
Private	
Number	
13622	
Unit	
1st Bn Lancashire Fusiliers	
Born	
Radcliffe, Lancashire 1896	
Enlisted	
Bolton, Lancashire	
Died	
Gallipoli, Turkey 8 September 1915	
Age	
18	
Grave or Memorial	
Azmak Cemetery, Suvla, Gallipoli, Turkey	

John William Nightingale

Bolton Journal and Guardian 30 July 1915

Killed in Gallipoli

The district of Darcy Lever has to record the death of another soldier who has sacrificed his life for his country's cause. Deceased is **Pte. J. W. Nightingale**, whose parents reside in Moaty-st. Pte. Nightingale enlisted in the Royal Dublin Fusiliers and was in training in Kent until May 4th. He was killed in Gallipoli on June 30th. Since his departure for training Nightingale never received a furlough. He resided at 29, Maze-st., and was a side-piecer at Messrs. Gray's, Darcy Lever Bridge Mills. He was a regular attender at Darcy Lever Wesleyan Church and Sunday school. Two other brothers of Nightingale's are serving in His Majesty's Forces.

Name	
Nightingale, John William	
Rank	
Private	
Number	
17472	
Unit	
1st Bn Royal Dublin Fusiliers	
Born	
Enlisted	
Bolton, Lancashire	
Died	
Gallipoli, Turkey 30 June 1915	
Age	
Grave or Memorial	
Helles Memorial, Gallipoli, Turkey	

Robert Norcross

Bolton Journal and Guardian 27 October 1915

Pte. R. NORCROSS, L.N.L. Regt., who was reported missing since August, 1915, is now officially reported killed. Prior to enlisting he was employed at the Horwich Loco Works. His parents reside at 21, Mercia-st., Bolton.

Robert was the son of Obadiah Norcross b.1855, a bobbin turner, and Ann Norcross née Moulding b.1856.

In 1901 Robert was living at 42a Cannon Street, Bolton with his parents and siblings James Moulding b.1878, John b.1880, Thomas b.1881, Peter b.1886, Margaret Jane b.1893, Richard b.1895 and Obadiah b.1900.

By the 1911 Census he was living at 32 Parkinson Street, Bolton with his parents and siblings Margaret and Richard.

Robert was working as a cotton spinner in 1911.

He was one of 10 children, one of whom had died by that point.

His little brother Obadiah was living with brother Thomas and his wife in Nottingham in 1911.

Name	Norcross, Robert
Rank	Private
Number	11930
Unit	6th Bn The Loyal North Lancashire Regiment
Born	Ribchester, Lancashire 1891
Enlisted	Bolton, Lancashire
Died	Gallipoli, Turkey 9 August 1915
Age	24
Grave or Memorial	Helles Memorial, Gallipoli, Turkey

James Norris

Bolton Journal and Guardian 14 July 1916

A Hero of the Dardanelles

After being reported missing since June 1915, the news has been received this week by his parents, who reside at 91, Nuttall-st., that their son, **Stoker James Norris**, was killed in the Dardanelles on June 4th, 1915. Stoker Norris had previously served five years in the Navy and had been on the reserve two years when the war broke out. He was immediately called up and joined the Royal Naval Division. He fought in the memorable retreat from Antwerp. Norris afterwards returned home on a short furlough. He was then sent to the Dardanelles in May, 1915, and after a month was reported missing. Prior to enlisting Stoker Norris worked at Messrs. Entwistle's mill, Washington-st. He was 27 years of age. He worshipped at the Saviour's Church, where he is on the Roll of Honour.

James was the son of Samuel Norris b.1862, a picker maker in a cotton mill, and Mary Jane Norris née Hardman b.1862.

James first appeared on the 1891 Census living at 88 Nuttall Street, Bolton with his parents and brothers William b.1887 and Samuel b.1890. His cousin, Alice Golding b.1889, was also part of the family.

By 1901 James had moved across the road to 91 Nuttall Street with his parents and brothers William, Samuel, Miles b1894, John b.1897 and Harold b.1899 and cousin Alice Golding.

James was serving in the Royal Navy by 1911.

His parents and brothers were still living at 91 Nuttall Street and had been joined by new children Harry b.1902, Mary Jane b.1904 and Ralph b.1907.

Alice Golding - at the age of 22 - was listed as their adopted daughter.

Name	Norris, James
Rank	Stoker 1st Class
Number	SS/105349 (RFR/B/4430)
Unit	Howe Bn Royal Naval Division
Born	Bolton, Lancashire 19 July 1888
Enlisted	4 July 1907
Died	Gallipoli, Turkey 4 June 1915
Age	26
Grave or Memorial	Helles Memorial, Gallipoli, Turkey

William Nuttall

Farnworth Weekly Journal 16 July 1915

FOOTBALLER KILLED

Mrs. Nuttall of 12, Thomas-st, Kearsley, has received official intimation of the death in action on June 19th, of her son, **Pte. William Nuttall** (18508) of the Inniskilling Fusiliers. The deceased who was aged 24, was unmarried, and enlisted in January at Farnworth. His last letter home was dated May 27th and was written on board a transport conveying him to the Dardanelles, before Gibraltar was reached. He was a collier at the Trencherbone mine of the Clifton and Kearsley Coal Company, as was also his brother Harry, who is with the Dublin Fusiliers. He attended St. Peter's Church, and used to be an active player in St. Peter's football team.

In his last letter Nuttall says: "I hope you are well at home. We are on a grand ship and and the weather is grand and very warm. This is our fourth day of sailing and we shall land in Gibraltar and anchor there for a few hours and then sail off for seven more days before we land. There is a piano on board and we have plenty of concerts, in fact we are singing the day over. I got a surprise the other day, for I landed on Tommy Myatt, who lives in George-st. There are about 60 on the ship from Bolton and round about, most of whom are from the Border Regiment, but we have a lot of other regiments. If our Harry has gone to the Dardanelles I am sure to meet him because they will be at the base at Alexandria. Don't worry about me, mother. I shall be back with you before long."

William was the son of William Nuttall b.1857, a coal miner, and Martha Nuttall née Berry b.1858.

In 1891 William was living at 66 Primrose Street with his parents and siblings Ann Berry b.1876, Mary Alice b.1878, John Thomas b.1880, Betsy b.1882, Susannah b.1895 and Harry b.1888.

William's father had died by 1901.

William appeared on the 1901 Census living at 12 Thomas Street, Kearsley with his mother and siblings Ann B, Mary Alice, John Thomas, Betsy, Susannah, Harry, Joshua b.1883 and James b.1894.

In 1911 William was still living at the same address with his mother and siblings Mary Alice, Susannah, Joshua and James.

At that time he was working as a piecer in a cotton mill.

His name is on Kearsley War Memorial.

Name	Nuttall, William
Rank	Private
Number	18508
Unit	1st Bn Royal Inniskilling Fusiliers
Born	Kearsley, Lancashire 1890
Enlisted	Farnworth, Lancashire
Died	Gallipoli, Turkey 19 June 1915
Age	24
Grave or Memorial	Twelve Tree Copse Cemetery, Gallipoli, Turkey

Name
O'Brien, John Joseph
Rank
Private
Number
16100
Unit
1st Bn
Royal Dublin Fusiliers
Born
Hulme, Manchester
1889
Enlisted
Farnworth, Lancashire
Died
Military Hospital,
Cairo, Egypt
10 June 1915
Age
26
Grave or Memorial
Cairo War Memorial
Cemetery,
Egypt

John Joseph O'Brien

Farnworth Weekly Guardian 15 June 1915

AN UNFINISHED LETTER

Mrs. O'Brien, of 86, Crompton-st, Farnworth, learns that her husband, **Pte. John Joseph O'Brien**, of the Dublin Fusiliers, has died from wounds received in action in the Dardanelles. Writing to Mrs. O'Brien from the Military Hospital, The Citadel, Cairo, Sister M. Howell says "You will have heard, before receiving my letter, the sad news of your husband's death, but I thought yo would like to hear a little more about him. I am enclosing a letter I found written to you and I am sure you will be pleased to receive it. Your husband was badly wounded with a piece of shrapnel and his leg was so badly crushed up that it had to be amputated below the knee. I cannot give you the date of his injury but he was brought here on June 9th. His leg was in a very bad condition and he himself very weak. The next day he was much worse and gangrene, generally known as mortification, set in. The doctors and sisters and all did their best but it was beyond our power and he died on June 11th** at 10-5 p.m. It will comfort you to know that the priest saw him before he died. May God comfort you and your children in your sad loss. Your husband has given his life for his home and country like so many more of our brave men. This war is so terrible." Private O'Brien had evidently intended to explain how he met with his wound, but his letter to his wife was unfinished. He says "I am in a poor condition for I am slightly wounded in the leg, but you must keep your heart up. I shall not be long before I am at home with you and the children. I had not long been in the trenches when I got done(?) and we lost heavily. I was one of the lucky ones. I got hit with shrapnel -" He had four other brothers serving their country: Pte. Owen O'Brien, Shropshire Light Infantry, who is at the front, Pte. Lewis* O'Brien, Lancashire Fusiliers, in training at Conway, Pte. Wm. O'Brien of the Inniskilling Fusiliers in France, and Pte James O'Brien of the South Lancashire Regiment, in training at Fulton, near Liverpool. Pte O'Brien has also two sons-in-law in the Army - Pte Wm. Mather, of the L.N.L., at Aldershot, Pte. J. Grimbley of the Lancashire Fusiliers, training in Yorkshire and a brother Pte. Joseph O'Brien of the Duke of Wellington's Own Regiment, in training at Halifax. There are also about 11 other relations serving.

John was the son of Louis (or Lewis*) O'Brien b.1858, a plumber, and Mary O'Brien née Cahill b.1861.

He first appeared on the 1891 Census living at 21 Park Place, Hulme, Manchester with his parents and siblings Florence b.1883, Owen b.1884, Louis* b.1885 and Mary B b.1890. John was working as a doffer in a cotton mill.

By 1901 he was living at 68 Crompton Street, Farnworth with his parents and siblings Agnes b.1883, Florence, Owen, Louis*, Mary B, William b.1891, Gertrude, b.1896, James b.1897, Annie b.1899 and Norah b.1901.

John married Alice Dudley at St James's Church, New Bury, Farnworth on 13 February 1909.

In 1911 the couple were living at 35 Stone Hill, Buckley Lane, Farnworth with their daughters Alice b.1909 and Maggie May b.1901. John was working as a collier / hewer.

A son, Albert, was born in 1913.

John's name is on Farnworth War Memorial.

*   Louis and Lewis are both used.

**CWGC gives 10 June as date of death.

Thomas O'Brien

Farnworth Weekly Guardian 23 July 1915

MISSING

Mrs. O'Brien, of 115 Bridgewater-st. has received official notification that her husband, **Private Thomas O'Brien**, of the Royal Dublin Fusiliers, was posted as missing after an engagement with the Mediterranean Expeditionary Force on June 4th. He enlisted on December 3rd., and after being at Dublin, he was drafted with his regiment to Sittingbourne, Kent, before going to the Dardanelles. He was employed as a hod carrier by Messrs. Coope Bros., Bank-st., Farnworth.

Thomas was the son of Patrick O'Brien b.1841, a labourer, and Mary O'Brien b.1843.

He first appeared on the 1881 Census living at Kent Street, Farnworth with his parents and siblings John b.1866, Julia b.1868, Mary b.1872, and Edward b.1881.

In 1891 he was living at 121 Bridgewater Street, Farnworth with his siblings Mary and Edward.

In 1901 the family were still living at the same address. Thomas was working as drawer in a coal mine.

Thomas married Mary Ann McAtee in 1905.

In 1911 the couple were living at 115 Bridgewater Street, Farnworth with their sons Thomas b.1906 and John b.1908.

Thomas was working as a bricklayer's labourer.

Thomas's name is on Farnworth War Memorial.

Name	
	O'Brien, Thomas
Rank	
	Private
Number	
	17474
Unit	
	1st Bn Royal Dublin Fusiliers
Born	
	Farnworth, Lancashire 1879
Enlisted	
	Farnworth, Lancashire
Died	
	Gallipoli, Turkey 4 June 1915
Age	
	36
Grave or Memorial	
	Helles Memorial, Gallipoli, Turkey

William Partington

Bolton Journal and Guardian 8 June 1919

In the Famous Fusiliers

News has been received that **Private Wm. Partington**, Mounted Infantry Section, 1st Lancashire Fusiliers, a single man whose widowed mother resides with her married daughter, Mrs. Speight, Fraser-st., died from wounds on January 5th. Deceased was the youngest of three brothers, the other two, Pte. H Partington R.F.A.,and Pte. J. Partington, L.N.L. being at present "somewhere" in France. Joining the Fusiliers at the age of 16, William spent five years in India, and on being transhipped to England twelve months ago, he enjoyed a short furlough at home before his Battalion, now immortalised by the famous "Lancashire landing", embarked for Gallipoli, The young hero, whose age was 23, was an old boy of Brownlow Fold Council School, where his name appears on the Roll of Honour. By a tragic coincidence, a letter was received by the same post which brought news of his death.

On the 1911 Census William was listed as serving as a private soldier with the Lancashire Fusiliers in India.

Name	
Partington, William	
Rank	
Private	
Number	
1681	
Unit	
1st Bn Lancashire Fusiliers	
Born	
Bolton, Lancashire c.1892	
Enlisted	
Bury, Lancashire	
Died	
Gallipoli, Turkey 5 January 1916	
Age	
23	
Grave or Memorial	
Lancashire Landing Cemetery, Gallipoli, Turkey	

Henry Parker

Henry's name is on Farnworth War Memorial.

Name	*Parker, Henry*
Rank	*Private*
Number	*652*
Unit	*6th Bn Royal Munster Fusiliers*
Born	*Farnworth, Lancashire c.1879*
Enlisted	*Farnworth, Lancashire*
Died	*Gallipoli, Turkey 9 August 1915*
Age	*36*
Grave or Memorial	*Helles Memorial, Gallipoli, Turkey*

Joseph Parker

Bolton Journal and Guardian 10 September 1915

Lost with the Royal Edward

Several Boltonians were on board the Royal Edward when she was torpedoed and sunk in the Mediterranean on the 13th August...

Word has been received from the Admiralty that **Private** (18318) **Jos. Parker**, 10th Border Regiment, is posted as "missing, believed drowned," by the sinking of the transport. He was a widower, living at 96, John Taylor-st., and leaves one child. He enlisted in November, and had been in training at Southend-on-Sea and in Essex. He has a brother in the Loyal North Lancashire Regiment, in training in Aldershot.

Name	
Parker, Joseph	
Rank	
Private	
Number	
18318	
Unit	
1st Bn Border Regiment	
Born	
Bolton, Lancashire 1875	
Enlisted	
Bolton, Lancashire 3 December 1914	
Died	
At sea 13 August 1915	
Age	
42	
Grave or Memorial	
Helles Memorial, Gallipoli, Turkey	

Joseph was the son of William Parker b.1843, a mechanic / machine fitter, and Alice Parker née Townsend b.1848.

Joseph first appeared on the 1881 Census living at 30 Coe Street, Bolton with his parents and sister, Margaret Townsend b.1870.

In 1891 Joseph was still living at 30 Coe Street with his parents and siblings Ada b.1884, Mary Jane b.1887 and James b.1890.

Joseph was working as a cotton piecer.

His mother died in 1900.

In 1901 the family were still living at the same address. Joseph was by then working as a coal miner.

Joseph married Sarah Jane Percival b.1880 at St Matthew's Church, Bolton on 17 May 1902.

He was employed as a collier at the time.

They had one daughter Alice b.1903. Sarah Jane died in 1906.

In 1911 Joseph was living as a boarder in Moorthorpe, Yorkshire and was working as a coal miner.

His daughter, was living as a boarder with the Rosbottom family at 34 Woodgate Street, Great Lever, Bolton.

By the time of his enlistment in the Army Joseph was living in Bolton again, at 4 Worsel Street. His Army medical examination recorded him as being 5' 8" and weighing 155 lbs.

He lost his life alongside hundreds of others when HMT Royal Edward was torpedoed by the German submarine UB-14 while en route from Alexandria to Lemnos. The ship was carrying 1367 officers and men destined for Gallipoli.

Joesph's daughter Alice was awarded a pension of 5/- a week.

Joseph Michael Philbin

Bolton Journal and Guardian 10 November 1916

Pte. JOSEPH PHILBIN, Loyal North Lancashire 42, Partridge-st., joined the Colours soon after war was declared, and whilst fighting in the Gallipoli campaign twelve months later was posted as wounded and missing. The wife and three children received no further tidings of him until, a few days ago, the military authorities reported that he must now be presumed to have lost his life. His name is on the St. Edmund's Roll of Honour. Philbin was 37 years of age, and prior to the war was a bricksetter's labourer in the employ of Messrs. Sparks and Hargreaves, Halliwell.

Joseph was the son of Michael Philbin b.1852, a bricklayer's labourer, and Ann Philbin née Early b.1854. Both parents were born on Merseyside.

Joseph first appeared on the 1881 Census living at 29 Back Kirk Street, Bolton with his parents and siblings Edward b.1873, Thomas b.1876 and Mary Ann b.1880.

By the 1891 Census Joseph was living at 12 Barkers Row Bootle, Lancashire with his parents and silings Edward, Mary Ann, John b.1883 and James b.1890. Thomas was living as a boarder in another part of Bootle in 1891.

Joseph married Margaret McDonald b.1879 in West Derby, Lancashire in 1897.

In 1901 the couple were living at 18 Sapphire Street, Wavertree, Liverpool with their son Michael b.1898. Joseph was working as a bricklayer's labourer.

On the 1911 Census they were shown living at 42 Partridge Street, Bolton with children Michael, Maria b.1902 and Joseph b.1905.

All three children were born in Liverpool.

Joseph was again employed as a bricklayer's labourer.

Name	Philbin, Joseph Michael
Rank	Private
Number	11856
Unit	6th Bn The Loyal North Lancashire Regiment
Born	Bolton, Lancashire 1878
Enlisted	Bolton, Lancashire
Died	Gallipoli, Turkey 10 August 1915
Age	37
Grave or Memorial	Helles Memorial, Gallipoli, Turkey

OUR
GLORIOUS
DEAD

THIS MEMORIAL WAS ERECTED
IN PROUD AND LOVING MEMORY
OF THE MEN OF
EGERTON, EAGLEY, DUNSCAR
AND BROMLEY CROSS
WHO FELL DURING THE GREAT WAR
1914 - 1918

LEST WE FORGET

To the
Everlasting Memory
of our Glorious Dead
1914-1918
Erected by
Eagley Mills Works
Employees

T. ALSOP .... PRIVATE
D. ANDREWS .... SERGEANT
H. ARCHER .... DRIVER
J.W. ATHERTON ..... PRIVATE
T. BALAH
J. BARBER
J. BENTHAM
J. BRADBURY
W. BIBBY
T. BORROMAN
W. BONE
T. BRIDGES .... L/ CORPORAL
H. V. BROWNHILL ... CORPORAL
S. BUNCOCK .... "
W. T. BURGESS .... PRIVATE
T. BURNS .... "
J. BURTON

Samuel Pickvance

Samuel's name appears on the Bolton Borough Roll of Honour.

Name
Pickvance, Samuel
Rank
Private
Number
2243
Unit
1st/5th Bn Manchester Regiment
Born
Enlisted
Died
Gallipoli, Turkey 6 August 1915
Age
Grave or Memorial
Helles Memorial, Gallipoli, Turkey

Horwich Loco Works War Memorial (left) on Chorley New Road, Horwich, was paid for by employees of the former Horwich Locomotive Works.

It was unveiled on 27 August 1921 by Mr George Hughes, chief mechanical engineer, and consists of a Carrara marble figure of a soldier on a Cornish granite pedestal.

Dunscar War Memorial (far left) is located at the junction of Blackburn Road and Darwen Road. The wedge-shaped plot of land enclosed by the roadways was known as 'Finger Post', and it was here that short services were held each Sunday evening during the First World War, after which the names of the most recent casualties from the local community were read out.

It was unveiled on 7 May 1921 by Lieut-Colonel J W Slater and takes the form of a bronze soldier with arms reversed on a pedestal of Bath stone.

John William Pitfield

John was the son of Walter Pitfield b.1872, a house painter and Ellen Pitfield née McGee b.1874.

John first appeared on the 1901 Census living at 6 Holden Street, Bolton with his parents and brother Charles Aloysious b.1899.

In 1911 they were living at 100 John Taylor Street, Bolton with additional children Benedict Joseph b.1905, Mary Magdeline b.1908 and Walter b.1909.

John was working as an apprentice fire grate fitter in 1911.

Another child, Wilfred A Pitfield, was born in 1913.

James Poole

Bolton Journal and Guardian 19 November 1915

Drowned with Mediterranean Expeditionary Force

Word has just been received by his wife that **Pte. James Poole**, 235, Bark-st., has been drowned whilst serving with the R.A.M.C. in Gallipoli. He was 31 years of age, and enlisted on March 2nd. After training at Lincoln he left England at the beginning of August. Before enlisting he was employed at the Swan Hotel. Three letters sent by him, the last of which was dated October 22nd, were received by his wife a few hours previous to the notification of his death, and another was received on Monday. He leaves a widow and one child. His brother Henry*, who is 22 years of age, and who resided with his parents in Deane-rd., has been reported missing in Gallipoli. He also was in the R.A.M.C.

James was the son of Henry Poole b.1853, an iron planer, and Emma Poole née Gaskin b.1863.

Emma was Henry's second wife. He married Emma in 1882.

James first appeared on the 1891 Census living at 66 Salisbury Street, Lenton, Nottingham with his parents and sisters Jane b.1874 and Ada b.1890.

By 1901 the family had moved to Bolton and James was living at 247 Bark Street with his parents and siblings Ada, Martha b.1892 and Henry b.1894.

James was at this point employed as an apprentice machine fitter.

James married Mary Hannah Banks at St Paul's Church, Deansgate, Bolton in 1908.

In 1911 the couple were living at 25 Leicester Street, Bolton with their daughter Ada b.1909. James was working as a barman in a public house.

* Henry Poole is not listed as having died in the First World War.

Name	
	Poole, James
Rank	
	Private
Number	
	56828
Unit	
	17th Stat. Hosp, Royal Army Medical Corps
Born	
	Radford, Nottingham, Nottinghamshire 1884
Enlisted	
	Bolton, Lancashire 2 March 1914
Died	
	At sea 28 October 1915
Age	
	31
Grave or Memorial	
	Helles Memorial, Gallipoli, Turkey

Name
Porter, Robert William
Rank
Sergeant
Number
1895
Unit
1st Bn
Lancashire Fusiliers
Born
Bradshaw, Nr Bolton, Lancashire
1895
Enlisted
Bury, Lancashire
Died
Gallipoli, Turkey
7 August 1915
Age
20
Grave or Memorial
Helles Memorial
Gallipoli, Turkey

Robert William Porter

Robert was the son of Thomas Porter b.1872, a railway passenger guard, and Mary Jane Porter née Dean b.1870.

In 1911 Robert was living at 1 Lathom Street, Bury, Lancashire with his parents and brother Thomas b.1898.

He was employed as a railway clerk.

His name is on the Lancashire and Yorkshire Railway War Memorial on Victoria Station, Manchester.

John Preston

John was the son of William Preston, a labourer, and Ann Preston b.1868.

John first appeared on the 1901 Census living at 6 Folds Court, Bolton with his mother and siblings Mary Elizabeth b.1890, Margaret Ann b.1893, William b.1895 and Helen b.1900.

John's mother Ann remarried to James Lowe in Bolton in 1905.

Ann died c.1910 and by 1911 John and his brother William were living at 57 Smith Street, Bolton with their stepfather and half-siblings Annie Lowe b.1906 and James Lowe b.1909.

John was working as a crofter in a bleachworks.

Name	Preston, John
Rank	Private
Number	2561
Unit	1st/7th Bn Lancashire Fusiliers
Born	Bolton, Lancashire 29 March 1897
Enlisted	Bury, Lancashire
Died	Gallipoli, Turkey 6 June 1915
Age	18
Grave or Memorial	Helles Memorial Gallipoli, Turkey

James Ratcliffe

Bolton Journal and Guardian 17 December 1915

Westhoughton Soldier Dies from Pneumonia

Mr. and Mrs. Seth Ratcliffe, 130, Church-st., Westhoughton, have been notified by the Preston military authorities that their son, **Pte. James Ratcliffe**, died of pneumonia on the 3rd inst., presumably in Gallipoli. Deceased, who was 21 years of age, and an only son, was of a very quiet disposition, and before enlisting was a "lasher" at the No. 2 Hewlitt Pit, Hart Common, belonging to the Wigan Coal and Iron Company. He joined the Army on January 4th last, when he enlisted in the 6th Battalion King's Own Royal Lancaster Regiment. He was home on furlough at the end of July prior to proceeding to the Mediterranean. Writing home a few weeks ago he stated that he was at Chocolate Hill, Suvla Bay.

James was son of Seth Ratcliffe b.1865, a tripe dealer, and Mary Ratcliffe b.1868.

James first appeared on the 1901 Census - as Nathaniel J Ratcliffe - living with his parents at 130 Church Street, Westhoughton.

His father was working as an agent for a burial society.

By the 1911 Census he was listed as James and was still living at 130 Church Street, Westhoughton with his parents.

His occupation was given as pit boy.

His name is on Westhoughton War Memorial.

Name	Ratcliffe, James
Rank	Private
Number	16839
Unit	6th Bn King's Own (Royal Lancaster Regiment)
Born	Leigh, Lancashire c.1894
Enlisted	Atherton, Lancashire 4 January 1915
Died	Gallipoli, Turkey 3 December 1915
Age	21
Grave or Memorial	Hill 10 Cemetery, Gallipoli, Turkey

Matthew Reddy

Bolton Journal and Guardian 28 May 1915

IN THE DARDANELLES

News has been received from the War Office by Mrs. Reddy, 8, Slater-st., that her son, **Pte. Matthew Reddy**, 1st Border Regiment, was killed in action in the Dardanelles on May 14th*. Reddy, who was a single man, has served eight years and five months in the Army, six years having been spent in India. He was one of a party that came from India at the New Year, and was granted four days' leave preparatory to going to the Dardanelles in February. Previous to joining the Army Reddy was a constant worshipper at St Mary's Catholic Church, and was in the old Bolton Volunteers for four years. He worked as a painter for Mr. Swarbrick, Chorley Old-rd.

Matthew was the son of John Reddy b.1847, a house painter, and Winifred D Reddy b.1848.

His parents were also listed on various Censuses as Matthew and Catherine / Direndow.

Matthew himself first appeared on the 1891 Census living at 6 Gleave Street, Bolton with his parents and siblings Mary b.1875, James b.1878, Alice b.1882 and Winifred b.1889. Another sister, Josephine was born in 1891 and their eldest son, John had been born in 1867.

Matthew's father John died in 1897.

In 1901 Matthew was an inmate of St. Joseph's Industrial School for Roman Catholic Boys in Longsight, Manchester. This was to all intents and purposes a juvenile prison for orphaned and delinquent children.

By 1911 he was serving as a private soldier with the Border Regiment in India.

Matthew's medical examination on enlistment in 1906 records him as being 8' 3 7/8" tall, weighing 114 lbs with a fair complexion, grey eyes and brown hair.

He attempted to obtain a free discharge from the Army in 1907 but was unsuccessful.

He served as a regimental bandsman in peacetime.

During his military career he notched up a long string of minor disciplinary offences - mostly for being late on parade - and a regimental report in 1914 described him as "A lazy man, Can do better if he tries. Careless and untidy." His character was also described as 'good'.

* *CWGC date of death is 28 April 1915*

Name	Reddy, Matthew
Rank	Private
Number	9204
Unit	1st Bn Border Regiment
Born	Bolton, Lancashire 1887
Enlisted	Bury, Lancashire 18 December 1906
Died	Gallipoli, Turkey 28 April 1915
Age	28
Grave or Memorial	Helles Memorial, Gallipoli, Turkey

Frederick Ribchester

Farnworth Weekly Journal 13 August 1915

FARNWORTH SOLDIER MISSING

Mrs. Ribchester of 11, Short-st., Farnworth has received intimation from the War Office that her son, **Lance Corpl. Fred Ribchester** (2474), of the 1st Lancashire Fusiliers, was posted as missing on June 29th, after an engagement in the Dardanelles. She has also had a letter from a young lady in London, who says that one of his companions in arms declares that he was killed. This statement remains to be verified, and Lance Corpl. Ribchester's sister has the assurance of the War Office that they will do their best to get further information. Ribchester has been in the Army for four years, and prior to this war was in India. He had two days furlough at home before going on active service. His father, Private John Ribchester, is with the National Reserve, guarding German prisoners at Leigh. He was wounded on May 17th in the Dardanelles, but only slightly. He had previously written to say:- "We are fighting at last, and such fighting I never dreamt of, or even thought possible. We effected a landing yesterday (Sunday). I don't know what date. I have lost count of everything. And what a landing it was too. They waited until the boats were about 30 yards from the beach and then the fun commenced. In my boat were about 40 men besides the sailors and a machine gun team, and all that got on land was myself and five men. The brutes had a Maxim trained on us and they took advantage of it too. And then snipers were ranged all along the top of the cliff. They, too, did a tremendous amount of damage. When the roll was called we found that 412 men, officers and N.C.O's were left out of the whole battalion. I am all right up to now, and if it lies in my power I always will be. I mean of course, to do my utmost and always to do my duty. To-day is Friday, and we have been in action continually since Sunday morning. We cannot grumble about our food - bully beef and those hard biscuits - but this morning I and three more chaps had quite a feed. I bagged a hare, pinched a ham-bone and with two tins of bully beef boxed up a fine stew." His last letter home, written on June 9th., was a pessimistic one. He said: "We leave tomorrow, June 10th., for the fighting again - my second time on earth. I cannot say very much, as I feel a bit upset about leaving tomorrow. Remember me to all kind friends who inquire after me."

Writing to his wife at 26-Northumberland-st, Farnworth Private H. Langan, also of the Lancashire Fusiliers, says, "I see that Ribchester has died. I daresay his mother will have got to know. If not tell her, and that I am very sorry. There are plenty of young men at home who are not married and ought to be made to fight. That they don't enlist shows that they must be a lot of cowards. Never mind, you and my mother can always say she had three sons who did their duty as young men ought to do."

Frederick was the son of John Ribchester b.1863, a carpenter and joiner, and Annie Ribchester née Aaron b.1861.

Frederick first appeared on the 1901 Census living at 9 Rawson Road, Farnworth with his parents and siblings Agnes b.1891, Mary Elizabeth b.1893, Jessie b.1897, John b.1899 and Frank James b.1900.

By 1911 he was living at 22 Cobden Street, Farnworth with his parents and siblings Jessie, Frank, John b.1903 and Horace b.1906.

Frederick was employed as a piecer in a cotton mill.

His name is on Farnworth War Memorial.

James Ritchie

James was the son of Thomas Ritchie and Mary C Ritchie.

He was living with his father at 184 Chorley Old Road, Bolton and working as a collier when he enlisted in the Army.

His Army medical examination recorded him as being 5' 7 1/4" tall.

His enlistment papers also list his siblings as Janet b.1898, Campbell b.1913 and Betty b.1915

Name	Ritchie, James
Rank	Private
Number	18198
Unit	1st Bn Border Regiment
Born	1895
Enlisted	Bolton, Lancashire 30 November 1914
Died	Gallipoli, Turkey 4 July 1915
Age	20
Grave or Memorial	Twelve Tree Copse Cemetery, Gallipoli, Turkey

1914 – 1918

TO THE GLORIOUS DEAD

IN
GRATEFUL MEMORY
OF THE MEN OF
BLACKROD
WHO GAVE THEIR LIVES
IN THE GREAT WAR

ROBERT ALKER
JOHN ANDERTON
HARRY ARMSTRONG
WILLIAM BAILEY
HERBERT BANKS
JOHN E BIRCHALL
FRANK BOLTON
THOMAS DOWLING
WILLIAM EARL
HARRY CAPPER
JAMES GERRARD
LEONARD GREEN
ARTHUR GREENHALGH
ROBERT S GREGORY
THOMAS HAMPSON
THOMAS E HARGREAVES
ROBERT HARGREAVES
RICHARD HART
ALBERT E MAYBURY
WILLIAM J MAYBURY
JOSEPH METCALFE
THOMAS MOSS
JAMES MULDOON
GEORGE A MOORE
JAMES OWEN
JOHN OWEN
OWEN OWEN
WILLIAM OWENS
JOHN C EGERTON
JAMES RODBURY
JOHN RIGBY
JOHN ROYCROFT
ISAAC H SILVER
ROBERT SPEAR
HARRY SUMNER
JOSEPH TOOTELL
THOMAS TURNBULL
JOSEPH WALSH
ALFRED WILKINSON
RALPH WILKINSON
JOSEPH WOOD
EGERTON L V WRIGHT
BENJAMIN YATES

THEIR NAME LIVETH
FOR EVERMORE.

TO THE GLORIOUS MEMORY OF
THE OFFICERS, N.C.O.S AND MEN
OF THE BOLTON ARTILLERY
WHO FELL DURING THE GREAT WAR
1914 – 1918
AND THE WORLD WAR
1939 – 1945

LEST WE FORGET

Edward Rimmer

Edward's name appears on the Bolton Borough Roll of Honour.

Name	Rimmer, Edward
Rank	Private
Number	2377
Unit	1st Bn Lancashire Fusiliers
Born	c.1883
Enlisted	
Died	Gallipoli, Turkey 25 April 1915
Age	32
Grave or Memorial	Helles Memorial, Gallipoli, Turkey

The Bolton Artillery Memorial in Nelson Square, Bradshawgate (left), was unveiled on 20 July 1920 by the **Duke of York** (the future King George VI) with **Robert Parkinson** (Mayor of Bolton 1919-21) leading the ceremonies.

It lists the names of just over 300 soldiers of the Battery who lost their lives in both World Wars - not those Bolton men who were killed while serving with other Artillery units.

Within the cenotaph itself is a shell case which contains copies of the Battery records from the First World War.

Blackrod War Memorial (far left) stands at the entrance to Blackrod Cemetery and is also in the form of a cenotaph constructed of Stancliffe stone.

It was unveiled on 29 March 1925 by **Mrs Mary Ann Wilkinson**.

Thomas Rothwell

Died from wounds.

Name	
Rothwell, Thomas	
Rank	
Private	
Number	
17246	
Unit	
6th Bn	
The Loyal North	
Lancashire Regiment	
Born	
Bolton, Lancashire	
Enlisted	
Bolton, Lancashire	
Died	
Gallipoli, Turkey	
12 August 1915	
Age	
Grave or Memorial	
Helles Memorial,	
Gallipoli, Turkey	

James Scott

Bolton Journal and Guardian 27 July 1915

FROM FRANCE TO DARDANELLES - NOW MISSING

Private J. Scott, of the 2nd Lancashire Fusiliers, is reported missing since the action on Gallipoli on June 10th. His home is at 20, Hewitt-st., and he has a wife and two children. An old soldier and a South African medallist, Private Scott was well-known locally, being employed as a postman in the Bolton area. He was in the reserve when the war broke out, went with his battalion to France, was severely wounded at the Marne battle, and recently joined a draft for the Dardanelles after a few weeks furlough in Bolton. A member of a notable soldiering family, Private Scott has a large circle of friends, all of whom are greatly concerned at the distressing news.

Bolton Journal and Guardian 8 October 1915

Bolton Reservist Reported Killed

Word has been received that **Private James Scott**, 1st Lancashire Fusiliers, who was reported missing after an engagement in Gallipoli on June 4th, is now reported killed. At the outbreak of war Private Scott was a postman. He was called up, and proceeded to France in September. After four months at the front he was invalided home with frostbite, and when better was despatched to the Dardanelles. He had only been in action four days when he was reported missing. Private Scott went through the South African war. He leaves a widow and three little children, who reside at 21, Hewitt-st., Bolton. He was a well known canary fancier and, a member of the Bolton Roller Canary Society and the Provincial Roller Club, and a successful exhibitor.

James was the son of James Scott b.1853, a cotton mill labourer, and Margaret Scott née Duffy b.1859.

His mother Margaret died in 1887.

James first appeared on the 1891 Census living at 2 Back Soho Street, Bolton with his widowed father and brothers Thomas b.1880, Robert b.1885 and Stephen b.1887.

James married Annie b.1883 in 1909.

In 1911 they were living at 20 Hewitt Street, Great Lever, Bolton with their children James b.1909 and Annie b.1910.

James was working as a postman at the time.

His name appears on the Roll of Honour at the main Post Office on Deansgate, Bolton.

Name	
	Scott, James
Rank	
	Private
Number	
	8762
Unit	
	1st Bn Lancashire Fusiliers
Born	
	Bolton, Lancashire 1882
Enlisted	
	Bolton, Lancashire
Died	
	Gallipoli, Turkey 4 June 1915
Age	
	32
Grave or Memorial	
	Helles Memorial, Gallipoli, Turkey

Name	
Seeler, Cornelius	
Rank	
Private	
Number	
17844	
Unit	
1st Bn	
Royal Dublin Fusiliers	
Born	
Ballymacelligott, Kerry, Ireland	
c.1882*	
Enlisted	
Bolton, Lancashire	
December 1914	
Died	
Gallipoli, Turkey	
29 June 1915	
Age	
33*	
Grave or Memorial	
Helles Memorial, Gallipoli, Turkey	

Cornelius Seeler

Bolton Journal and Guardian 30 July 1915

KILLED IN GALLIPOLI

News has been received that **Pte. Cornelius Seeler**, of the Royal Dublin Fusiliers was killed in action in Gallipoli on June 29th. Pte. Seeler enlisted in December, and never had a leave except a few days to attend the funeral of his child. Prior to enlisting he was employed by Messrs. Partington and Co., builders and contractors. He was a worshipper at St. Patrick's Catholic Church. His Bolton address was 9, Hengist-st., Tonge Fold, and he leaves a widow and five children.

Cornelius appeared on the 1911 Census living as a boarder at 55 Matthew Street, Bolton in the household of Michael and Annie Kennedy.

He was employed as a sewerage labourer.

Cornelius married Sarah Jane Cotterell née Peart in Bolton in 1913. She was a widow with four young children at the time.

The couple had two more daughters, Mary C b.1913 and Sarah J b.1914. Both died in infancy.

* *A Cornelius Seeler, born in Ireland, appeared on the 1901 Census living in Bristol and working as a grain porter but his age then was given as 25 - ie b.1876.*

Robert Selkirk

Bolton Journal and Guardian 19 May 1916

Fought in Gallipoli

Very little hope is entertained of hearing anything further of **Pte. Robert Selkirk** (16438), Royal Dublin Fusiliers, a Boltonian who fought in Gallipoli, but information of any kind would be welcomed by his sister, Mrs Gaskell of 65, Parrott-st. he enlisted in the early stages of the war, and after a period of training at the Curragh Camp, sailed for the Mediterranean on July 7th. In January the military authorities reported that he was wounded and missing, and since then all efforts to trace him have been in vain. Aged 30, and married, he was formerly a labourer at Messrs. Peter Crook's Ramsbottom-st. mills.

Bolton Journal and Guardian 9 June1916

Mill Worker Killed

A War Office message following upon one in which **Pte. R. Selkirk** (16438), of the Dublin Fusiliers, was reported wounded and missing, has been received by his wife at 13, Tyson-st., Deane-rd., to the effect that he is most likely killed. Selkirk, who was 30 years of age, enlisted in November, 1914, and after training at the Curragh, Ireland, was sent to the Dardanelles. Up to Joining the Colours he worked for Messrs. J. Crook and Sons, cotton spinners, Deane-rd., and attended Emmanuel Day and Sunday School, where he was on the Roll of Honour.

Robert was the son of Charles Selkirk b.1841, a joiner, and Betsy Selkirk née Walker b.c.1843.

Robert first appeared on the Census in 1901 living at 11 Edward Street, Bolton with his widowed mother and siblings Charles b.1873 and Mary Ellen b.1877.

He had two older brothers no longer present in 1891 - John Thomas b.1864 and Joseph Henry b.1866

In 1901 he was still living at 11 Edward Street with his mother and was employed as a piecer in a cotton mill.

Robert married Mary Anne Smith at Emmanuel Church, Bolton in 1907.

The couple were living at 110 Pen Street, Bolton in 1911. They had had one child by then but it had died in infancy.

Robert was still working as a piecer in a cotton mill.

Name	
	Selkirk, Robert
Rank	
	Private
Number	
	16438
Unit	
	6th Bn Royal Dublin Fusiliers
Born	
	Bolton, Lancashire 1885
Enlisted	
	Bolton, Lancashire
Died	
	Gallipoli, Turkey 10 August 1915
Age	
	30
Grave or Memorial	
	Helles Memorial, Gallipoli, Turkey

William Sharples

Farnworth Weekly Journal 12 November 1915

FARNWORTH SOLDIER KILLED

Mrs. Sharples, 67, Glynne-st., on Monday received official intimation that her husband, **Pte. Wm. Sharples** (18347) of the 6th L.N.L. Regiment, was killed in action at the Dardanelles on October 11th. She had received three letters from him the same morning., the last written on October 9th and posted the day he died, stating that he was in the trenches for the first time, but it was quiet except for the echoing of a few shots now and then. "I pray to God to bring me back safe home to you." he said. When he wrote previously, on September 24th he was stationed on a hill, though within reach of the guns. The deceased, who was 28 years of age, enlisted on November 21st of last year, and went to the Dardanelles from Felixstowe on August 28th. He was engaged in the winding department of Messrs. T. Barnes and Co.'s No. 2 Mill, Gladstone-rd, but for a time worked at Messrs. Wallwork and Sussum's mill. He is on the roll of honour at St. George's School, Plodder-lane, and the King-st Workingmen's Mission, attending the latter place since his marriage, and Mrs. Sharples has received a sympathetic letter from the officials of the Mission. His brother, who enlisted with me in the 3rd L.N.L., has gone to Serbia, while Mrs. Sharpies's sister's husband, Private Arthur Tyson, has been a prisoner of war in Germany for 14 months.

William was the son of Henry Sharples b.1861, a pit brow labourer, and Mary Alice Sharples née Allen b.1861.

William first appeared on the 1891 Census living at 23 Water Lane Street, Radcliffe with his parents and siblings John b.1886 and Nancy b.1890.

William's mother died in 1900 and in 1901 he was living at 19 Victoria Street, Farnworth with his father and siblings John, Nancy and Margaret b.1892.

Aged 13 William was already working as a little piecer in a cotton mill.

William married Marian Jones b.1887 at St James's Church, New Bury, Farnworth on 6 December 1909.

In 1911 the couple were living at 10 Cross Street, Farnworth with two boarders.

William was by then employed as a spinner in a cotton mill.

His name is on Farnworth and Little Lever War Memorials.

William Robert Simpson

Bolton Journal and Guardian 10 September 1915

MISSING IN GALLIPOLI

Information has been received in Bolton that **Pte. William R. Simpson** (19139), 1st Battalion, Border Regiment, has been wounded in the Dardanelles. Pte. Simpson, who resided at 181, Morris Green-lane, was a regular attender at Morris Green Sunday school, and was also a prominent football player. His father is serving in the King's R.L.I., and is at present stationed in the Isle of Man.

Bolton Journal and Guardian 17 September 1915

Borderer Dies from Wounds

The roll of Bolton's gallant dead has been further augmented by the name of **Pte. W. R. Simpson** (19139), 1st Battalion Border Regiment, who was wounded in Gallipoli. He was removed to the Bombay Presidency General Hospital, Alexandria, suffering from a serious wound in the body, but he later developed dysentery, and though it was hoped that he might recover, official notice of his death was received yesterday morning. Pte. Simpson, who enlisted in January, lived with his mother at 181, Morris Green-lane, but he married in May, and left for his training ground two days later. His wife lives at 17, Gordon-street, Daubhill. He was a regular attender at Morris Green Sunday School, and was a prominent player in connexion with the school football team. The brave young fellow was a side piecer at the Dove Spinning Mill. His father is serving in the King's R.L.I., and is at present stationed in the Isle of Man.

William was the eldest son of Thomas Edmund Simpson b.1868, a labourer for Bolton Corporation, and Lilian Simpson née Cooey b.1873.

He first appeared on the 1901 census living at 39 Durham Street, Bolton with his parents and brothers Thomas Edmund b.1898 and John b.1900.

By 1911 the William was living at 181 Morris Green Lane, Bolton with his parents, brothers Thomas Edmund and John and sisters Lilian b.1903 and Evelyn b.1909.

William married Elizabeth Ormston b.1896 at St Philip's Church Bolton in May 1915

His medical examination on enlistment in the Army recorded him as being 5' 3" tall and weighing 117 lbs.

Name	
Simpson, William Robert	
Rank	
Private	
Number	
19139	
Unit	
1st Bn Border Regiment	
Born	
Bolton, Lancashire 1892	
Enlisted	
Bolton, Lancashire	
Died	
Alexandria, Egypt 3 September 1915	
Age	
23	
Grave or Memorial	
Chatby Military and War Memorial Cemetery, Alexandria, Egypt	

Walter Alfred Singleton

Bolton Journal and Guardian 8 October 1915

Corporal Walter Singleton Dies from Enteric at the Dardanelles

Information has been received by his wife at 70, Eustace-st., Great Lever, that **Corpl. Alfred Singleton**, of the Army Veterinary Corps, has died of enteric fever* in the Dardanelles. Corpl. Singleton was well-known in the Bolton District as a former master baker, and later as a photographer. For many years he was a partner with his late brother, William, in an old established bakery and provision business in Bradshawgate founded by their father. After leaving the Bradshawgate business he took up photography, which had long been his hobby, and quickly developed a connexion, especially with the press. After the outbreak of war he enlisted at the Town Hall in the A.S.C., and later transferred to the Veterinary Corps, popularly known as the Blue Cross. In civil life he always took an interest in horses, and was well-known in Lancashire shows as a judge both of animals and also in the bread class. He leaves a widow and five children.

Walter was the son of Thomas Singleton b.1819, a bread baker, and Ann (later known as Nancy) Singleton b.1832.

Walter first appeared on the 1871 Census living with his parents at 73 Bradshawgate with his parents and siblings Elizabeth b.1853, Thomas C b.1855, William b.1858 and Cuthbert b.1860. The household also included a live-in domestic servant. Thomas's occupation is given as provision dealer. For some reason Mrs Singleton is listed as Ann.

The family were still at the same address in 1881 and the family business was by then bread baking. Alfred was living with his parents and brothers William and Cuthbert. Walter (listed as Alfred) was employed as a van boy (probably in the bakery business. The household also included to bakery workers and two domestic servants.

Walter married Annie Margaret Jones b.1867 in Bolton in 1886.

In 1891 the couple were living at 90 Dorset Street, Bolton with their children Minnie b.1887 Walter Stewart b.1888 and Jessie b.1890. The family have a live-in domestic servant. Walter is listed as being a Master Baker and flour dealer.

By 1901 the family were living at 7 Hilden Street, Bolton with their children Minnie, Walter Stewart, Jessie, William Jones b.1891 and Annie Clara b.1894.

Walter was absent from the 1911 Census but Annie Margaret and children Walter Stewart, Jessie, William Jones and Annie Clara were living at 70 Eustace Street, Bolton.

* Typhoid

Name	Singleton, Walter Alfred
Rank	Corporal
Number	SE/4154
Unit	16th Veterinary Section Army Veterinary Corps
Born	Bolton, Lancashire 1864
Enlisted	Bolton, Lancashire
Died	Gallipoli, Turkey3 September 1915
Age	50
Grave or Memorial	Helles Memorial, Gallipoli, Turkey

Joseph Smith

Bolton Journal and Guardian 4 June 1915

Another Dardanelles Hero

Bolton and district men have been in the thick of the fighting in the Dardanelles, and the casualty roll is exceptionally heavy. Every day brings news of more local soldiers being killed or wounded in the terrible conflicts with the Turks in the Gallipoli Peninsula. The latest hero to lose his life is **Pte. J. Smith**, Po. S. 714 Royal Marine Light Infantry. He was serving with the Portsmouth Battalion in the Royal Naval Division. In peace times he lived at 1, Percival-st.

Joseph was the son of William James Smith b.1858, a cooper, and Emily Smith née Palin b.1865.

Joseph first appeared on the 1891 Census living at 11 Fairfield Street, Bolton with his parents and brother James Blundell b.1889.

By 1901 Joseph's father was living apart from Emily at 2 Fleet Street, Bolton with his unmarried housekeeper Mary Wood and her daughter Jane b.1900.

In 1901 Joseph was living at 1 Richmond Place, Bolton with his mother and brothers James Blundell, George Sydney Herbert b.1892 and William James b.1900. His mother Emily was working as a charwoman.

Joseph's father was was still absent from the family home on the 1911 Census. Joseph (listed as Joe) was living with his mother and brothers at 1 Percival Street, Bolton.

He was employed as a side piecer in a cotton mill.

Name	
	Smith, Joseph
Rank	
	Private
Number	
	PO/714/S
Unit	
	Portsmouth Bn Royal Naval Division Royal Marine Light Infantry
Born	
	Bolton, Lancashire 1890
Enlisted	
Died	
	Gallipoli, Turkey 3 May 1915
Age	
	25
Grave or Memorial	
	Helles Memorial, Gallipoli, Turkey

Peter Smith

Bolton Journal and Guardian 24 September 1915

Missing in Gallipoli

A well-known Breightmet soldier, Private Peter Smith (9299) of the 9th Lancashire Fusiliers, has been posted as missing since an engagement in Gallipoli on August 21st. He was a single man, 33 years of age, and lived with his sister, Mrs. Seed at 972, Bury-rd., Breightmet. In civil life he worked as a collier at Coney Green Collieries, Black Lane. He had lived in Breightmet all his life and was well-known in the district.

Peter was the son of Adam Smith b.1839, a labourer, and Betsy Smith née Lord b.1842.

Peter first appeared on the 1891 Census living at 649 Bury new Road, Breightmet, Bolton with his parents and brothers Joseph b.1872, John b.1875 and Robert b.1877.

The two older daughters, Mary Jane b.1865 and Alice A b.1869 had left home by 1891.

By 1901 Peter was living at 92 Bury New Road with his brothers John and Robert in the household of his sister Mary Jane, her husband Charles Seed and their three children. He was employed as a coal hewer.

In 1911 he was still living with his sister, her husband and their 8 children at 972 Bury Road, Bolton.

He was then working as a coal miner.

Name	
Smith, Peter	
Rank	Private
Number	9299
Unit	9th Bn Lancashire Fusiliers
Born	Breightmet, Bolton, Lancashire 1882
Enlisted	Bury, Lancashire
Died	Gallipoli, Turkey 21 August 1915
Age	33
Grave or Memorial	Helles Memorial, Gallipoli, Turkey

Thomas Spencer

Thomas was the son of Henry Spencer b.1847, a cotton spinner, and Mary Spencer née Threlfall b.1848

Thomas first appeared on the 1881 Census living at 84 Aqueduct Street, Preston, Lancashire with his parents and siblings Anne J b.1867, Andrew b.1869, Arthur b.1872, Betsy b.1874, Jessie b.1876 and Mary b.1878.

In 1891 Thomas was living at 78 Brook Street with his parents and siblings Betsy, Jessie, Mary and Robert b.1893.

Thomas married Ada Clayton at St Bartholomew's Church, Bolton on 15 December 1900.

In 1901 they were living at 35 Channing Street, Bolton with two of Ada's sisters.

Thomas was employed as a cotton spinner.

By 1911 Thomas and Ada were living at 31 Woodfield Street, Great Lever, Bolton with their children Robert b.1902 and Mary b.1904.

Name	
Spencer, Thomas	
Rank	
Private	
Number	
19519	
Unit	
6th Bn The Loyal North Lancashire Regiment	
Born	
Preston, Lancashire c.1880	
Enlisted	
Bolton, Lancashire	
Died	
Gallipoli, Turkey 12 November 1915	
Age	
35	
Grave or Memorial	
Green Hill Cemetery, Gallipoli, Turkey	

Thomas Stallard

Bolton Journal and Guardian 24 December 1915

On St. Paul's, Astley Bridge, Roll of Honour

The chaplain of a section of the 38th Brigade Mediterranean Force writes to Mrs. Stallard, 29, Grasmere-st.: "It is with deep regret that I write to inform you that your son died of wounds this morning (Dec. 3rd). It is indeed very sad, as he was such a fine lad, and so young." **Pte. Thomas Stallard** (18905), 3rd South Lancashire Regiment, was aged 17 years. He sailed to the Dardanelles on Nov. 14th, after just seven months training at Blundellsands, Prior to enlisting he was employed in the Warehouse at Messrs. Greenhalgh and Shaw. He will be remembered as an old boy of Chalfont-st school, where his name appears on the Roll of Honour, and former comrades of the Astley Bridge Boys' Brigade will share the great sorrow that has fallen upon the deceased's family. Stallard was also associated with St. Paul's Church and Sunday School. His friend, Pte. Sam Roberts, resident in the same district, was wounded in the left shoulder three days after their arrival in Gallipoli.

Thomas was the son of George Stallard b.1873, a fish salesman, and Martha Stallard née Gardener b.1873.

He first appeared on the 1901 Census living at 607 Blackburn Road, Bolton with his parents and sister Ethel b.1900. His father was then a greengrocer / fruiterer.

By 1911 Thomas was living at 29 Grasmere Street, Bolton with his parents and siblings Ethel, Fred b.1905 and Mary Ann b.1903.

Thomas claimed he was 19 years and 200 days old on his Army enlistment form in April 1915.

His occupation was given as cop packer.

His medical examination recorded him as being 5' 1 1/6" tall and weighing 106 lbs.

He was admonished for playing football in barracks shortly after he joined up.

He died from wounds received in action.

Name	Stallard, Thomas
Rank	Private
Number	18594
Unit	6th Bn South Lancashire Regiment
Born	Bolton, Lancashire 1898
Enlisted	Great Crosby, Lancashire 14 April 1915
Died	Gallipoli, Turkey 3 December 1915
Age	17
Buried	Hill 10 Cemetery, Gallipoli, Turkey

George Edward Stockham

Bolton Journal and Guardian 11 June 1915

AMBULANCE HERO DEAD

News has reached Bolton that **Private Geo. Edward Stockham**, of the Royal Naval Auxiliary Sick Berth Res., who was awarded the Distinguished Service Medal for work in the Dardanelles, has died of his wounds. Much sympathy has been extended to Mrs. Stockham, who resides at 31 Mercia-st., with her six children, the youngest of whom was born two days after Stockham left Bolton with the first contingent of St. John Ambulance men sent out by Corps-Supt. F. Lomax on August 5th. Stockham, who is a native of Bristol, has been associated with ambulance work for 14 years, taking his first-aid certificate in 1901, and when he came to Trinity-st. Station some years ago as foreman cleaner in the carriage and wagon department he joined the L. and Y. ambulance centre, continuing under the instruction of Dr. J. Johnston, of Lostock. He afterwards joined the Bolton Corps of the St. John Ambulance Brigade, and under its auspices went to Chatham last August. After service at various places in England and at the siege of Antwerp he went out to the Dardanelles in February, and was seriously wounded on May 17th. What was the nature of his conduct on that occasion is not known, but it secured him the D.S.M. and the honour of being the second ambulance man to be decorated during the war, the other being Sergt. E. Walch, also of Bolton. His wounds were of a particularly serious nature, and both his feet had to be amputated. When this sad fact was told to Mrs. Stockham she recalled his last conversation with her when he said he would rather be killed than return to be a burden upon her, and she had remarked that death was what he would have chosen in the circumstances.

George was the son of William Henry Stockham b.1851, a haulier, and Alice Matilda Stockham née Sainsbury b.1849.

George married Mary Kitt at St James's Church, Higher Broughton, Salford in 1896.

In 1901 they were living at 40 Harrietta Street, Broughton with their daughters Gladys b1897 and Mildred b.1900.

By 1911 they were living at 21 Meadow Street, Wigan with additional children Thirza b.1902, George Edward b.1905 and Alice b.1907. He was then working as a railway cleaner.

Their youngest daughter, Mona, was born in Bolton in 1914.

Citation to award of Distinguished Service Medal in London Gazette 2 July 1915:

"During the night of May 9th-10th, in operations South of Achi Baba, worked splendidly under fire to recover wounded until himself severely wounded."

His name is on the Lancashire and Yorkshire Railway War Memorial on Victoria Station, Manchester.

Name	Stockham, George Edward
Rank	Junior Reserve Attendant
Number	M/9781
Unit	Plymouth Bn Royal Naval Division, Royal Naval Auxiliary Sick Berth Reserve
Born	Bristol, Gloucestershire 28 Jun 1874
Enlisted	9 August 1914
Died	Alexandria, Egypt 31 May 1915
Age	40
Grave or Memorial	Alexandria (Chatby) Military and War Cemetery, Egypt

Harry Tatlow

Bolton Journal and Guardian 21 July 1916

Rugby Footballer Killed

Pte. Harry Tatlow, son of the late Mr. J. T. Tatlow and Mrs. Tatlow, of Ravenstone, 9, Lightburn-avenue, Bolton, is now reported killed in action on or about June 5th, 1915, in Gallipoli. Pte. Tatlow, who was well known in Horwich, where his family resided for many years, was 24 years of age. He was born at Horwich, and went to Rivington and Blackrod Grammar School, later to the Leamington High School, and finished his education at Bolton Grammar School. On leaving school he joined the L. and Y. Railway staff at Hunts Bank, Manchester, and was in the traffic department when he joined the Colours. He was for many years actively interested in the Boy Scout movement, and was Scoutmaster of the 2nd Horwich Patrol. For Several years he was a playing member of the Manchester Rugby "A" team. He was keen to join up on the outbreak of war, and entered the 6th Manchesters with several of his football team, early in September, 1914.

Harry was the son of James Teare Tatlow b.1846, a railway accountant, and Martha Tatlow née Hughes b.1851.

James had had an earlier career as a master builder in Wolverhampton but had moved to Horwich by 1890 to join the town's booming locomotive manufacturing industry. The couple had also had three older children - Jessie Denchfield b.1869, Arthur Higdon b.1870 and Charles Edmund b.1876.

Harry first appeared on the 1901 Census living at Ravenstone, 49 Victoria Road, Horwich with his parents and siblings Alice Mary b.1874, Frank James b.1879 and Gertrude Martha b.1889. The family also employed a live-in domestic servant.

By 1911 Harry was living alone with his parents (and a live-in domestic servant) at 49 Victoria Road, Horwich.

His occupation was listed as railway clerk.

His name is on the Lancashire and Yorkshire Railway War Memorial on Victoria Station, Manchester.

Name
Tatlow, Harry
Rank
Private
Number
2477
Unit
1st/6th Bn Manchester Regiment
Born
Horwich, Lancashire 1892
Enlisted
Manchester
Died
Gallipoli, Turkey 5 June 1915
Age
24
Grave or Memorial
Helles Memorial, Gallipoli, Turkey

George Taubman

Farnworth Weekly Guardian 30 July 1915

ANOTHER FARNWORTH SOLDIER KILLED

Word has been received at the Farnworth and Kearsley Gas Works of the death of one of the stokers, **Pte. George Taubman**, who enlisted about December in the Dublin Fusiliers, from 27, Elizabeth-st., Farnworth. He is a native of the Isle of Man, to which his wife went after he had joined the forces. He visited the works a few months ago looking the picture of health. His father, writing from 3, Hanover-place, Douglas, I.O.M., on July 22nd, says: "I am very sorry to inform you that my son George died of wounds received on June 28th, whilst in action. We got word last night from the War office." Deceased was with the Mediterranean Expeditionary Force. Mr H. Pickford, manager of the works, has written on behalf of the men to Mr. Taubman expressing the sorrow with which they had received this information, and extending their sympathy to the relatives.

Farnworth Weekly Guardian 6 August 1915

GAS STOKER KILLED

Private Geo. Taubman, of the Dublin Fusiliers who enlisted about December from the Farnworth and Kearsley as Works died, as stated last week, on June 28th, from wounds he received whilst in action in the Dardanelles. He had been engaged as a stoker for some winters, and it was his habit during the summer months to work on the sea. His wife, with three children, left 27 Elizabeth-st, Farnworth, about Easter to join her parents, Mr. and Mrs. Devereaux (sic) at 5 Mucklegate, Douglas, Isle of Man, of which Taubman was also a native.

George married Edith Jane Devereau b.1887 at St George's, Douglas, Isle of Man on 2 December 1908.

In 1911 the couple were living at 15 Heywood Place, Douglas, Isle of Man with their daughter May b.1910.

George was working as a steamship fireman for the Isle of man Steam Packet Co.

They also had twin sons, George Howard and John Joseph O'Connor b.1913 and another daughter, Dora b.1915, all born in Farnworth.

George's name is on Farnworth War Memorial.

Name	
Taubman, George	
Rank	
Private	
Number	
17397	
Unit	
1st Bn Royal Dublin Fusiliers	
Born	
Douglas, Isle of Man 1885	
Enlisted	
Farnworth, Lancashire	
Died	
Alexandria, Egypt 28 June 1915	
Age	
30	
Grave or Memorial	
Alexandria (Chatby) Military and War Cemetery, Egypt	

Norman Thompson

Bolton Journal and Guardian

Killed in Gallipoli Fighting

Many of Bolton's sons have played a noble part in the severe fighting in the Dardanelles, and already a number of them have lost their lives, whilst others have been seriously wounded. News is to hand that **Corporal Norman Thompson**, attached to the 1st Battalion, Lancashire Fusiliers, who suffered heavily as a landing party, was killed on May 11th*, He is the son of the late Mr. Walton Thompson, Horace-st., and was 25 years of age. He is a single man and has been in the Army about six years, and had served three years in India. He spent a short furlough in Bolton at new Year, prior to going to the Dardanelles early in March.

Norman was the son of Walton Thompson b.1861, a stone mason, and Hannah Thompson née Hadfield b.1862.

Norman first appeared on the 1891 Census living at 46 Cellini Street, Bolton with his parents and siblings Harry Walton b.1886, Thomas b.1888 and Minnie Martha b.1890. His father was wrongly listed as 'Walter' on the Census return.

Minnie Martha died in infancy c.1892.

In 1901 he was living at 95 Oxford Grove, Bolton with his parents and siblings Harry Walton, Thomas, Elsie b.1893, Emma b.1895, Hannah Rachel b.1897 and Walton Clare (a son) b.1901.

By 1911 Norman was serving in the Army in India.

Norman's parents were living at 14 Nut Street, Halliwell, Bolton with children Harry Walton, Elsie, Hannah Rachel, Walton Clare, Frank b.1904 and Tilley b.1907.

* *Death recorded as 25 April on CWGC.*

Name	
Thompson, Norman	
Rank	
Corporal	
Number	
2162	
Unit	
1st Bn Lancashire Fusiliers	
Born	
Bolton, Lancashire 1889	
Enlisted	
Bury, Lancashire	
Died	
Gallipoli, Turkey 25 April 1915	
Age	
26	
Grave or Memorial	
Helles Memorial, Gallipoli, Turkey	

Albert Thornley

Bolton Journal and Guardian 10 September 1915

Lost with the Royal Edward

Several Boltonians were on board the Royal Edward when she was torpedoed and sunk in the Mediterranean on the 13th August...

Another Bolton soldier to be reported "missing, believed drowned" is **Pte. Albert Thornley**, of the King's Own Scottish Borderers, who enlisted in January. He was 20 years of age, and lodged with Mrs. Hulme at 4, Pool-terrace, Smithills. He was brought up at Eden's Orphanage. He was a capable swimmer, and gained the certificate of the Royal Humane Society in 1905. As a boy he attended the Saviour's Church, where he obtained many prizes for religious knowledge. Prior to enlisting he was employed at Messrs' R. H. Ainsworth, Son and Co., Limited's croft, Halliwell. He was a regular attender at the Smithills Chapel, where he was a member of the choir, and a Sunday school teacher. He played at cricket several times for Christ Church, Heaton, and is on their roll of honour, which contains the names of about 20 members of about 40 on the club's books. He also played at football for St. Peter's. He wrote to Mrs. Hulme from Malta, enclosing a photograph of the Royal Edward, and promising to write upon arrival at the Dardanelles. His death is keenly felt by those who knew him, for he was a most genial and respected young man.

Albert was the son of Richard Baxter Thornley b.1869, a millwright, and Alice Thornley née Hart b.1869.

Albert first appeared on the 1901 Census living at 105 Ellesmere Street with his parents and siblings Margaret b.1896, Richard Baxter b.1898 and James b.1900.

Albert's father died in 1903. His mother, Alice, remarried to Mark Wadsworth in Bolton in 1906.

By 1911 Albert, his brother James and sister Lily b.1902 were were living at 110 Gibraltar Street, Bolton with their uncle Henry Holt and aunt Amelia Holt née Thornley.

Albert was at that time employed as a crofter in a bleachworks.

Albert's other brother Richard Baxter Thornley and sister Margaret were inmates of Eden's Orphanage, Astley Bridge, Bolton in 1911.

There was also another sister, Alice.

Albert's medical examination on enlisting in the Army recorded him as being 5' 8" tall and weighing 154 lbs.

He lost his life alongside hundreds of others when HMT Royal Edward was torpedoed by the German submarine UB-14 while en route from Alexandria to Lemnos. The ship was carrying 1367 officers and men destined for Gallipoli.

Name	
Thornley, Albert	
Rank	Private
Number	19188
Unit	1st Bn Border Regiment
Born	Bolton, Lancashire 1894
Enlisted	Bolton, Lancashire 9 January 1915
Died	At sea 13 August 1915
Age	20
Grave or Memorial	Helles Memorial, Gallipoli, Turkey

Name	
Tickle, Richard	
Rank	
Private	
Number	
11841	
Unit	
6th Bn	
The Loyal North	
Lancashire Regiment	
Born	
Heaton, Bolton,	
Lancashire	
1895	
Enlisted	
Horwich, Lancashire	
24 August 1914	
Died	
Gallipoli, Turkey	
27 August 1915	
Age	
20	
Grave or Memorial	
Holy Trinity Church,	
Horwich, Lancashire	

Richard Tickle

Two Horwich Soldiers Killed

Mr. and Mrs. Christopher Coupes (sic), 17 Smeaton-st., Horwich, have received an intimation from the War Office that their son, Private Mark Coupes (11842), of the 6th Battalion, L.N.L. Regiment was killed in the Dardanelles on August 10th. Pte. Coupes was 20 years of age, and enlisted on the 24th of August last year. After having been in training at Salisbury, Winchester and Aldershot, he went to the Dardanelles in June last. Deceased was employed as an engine cleaner at the Loco. Works prior to enlisting. He was also a fairly well-known footballer and billiard player. In connexion with his football capabilities he recently won a medal given by the officers of his company. He was well-known in Horwich, and joined the army at the same time as another soldier, who has given his life for his country, **Pte. Richard Tickle**, whose regimental number was 11841, whilst Pte. Coupes was 11842.

Richard was the son of Richard Tickle b.1867, a spring smith's striker at Horwich Loco Works, and Sarah Ellen Tickle née Derbyshire b.1866.

Richard first appeared on the 1901 Census living at 1606 Chorley Old Road, Heaton, Bolton with his parents and older brother John b.1891.

By 1911 the family were living at 23 Barlow Street, Horwich.

Richard was then working as a labourer in a brick and tile works while his brother John was employed as a boiler maker's helper at Horwich Loco Works.

Richard died of wounds received in action.

His name is on the Horwich Loco Works War Memorial.

Thomas Tither

Bolton Journal and Guardian 3 September 1915

Westhoughton Soldier Killed

Official news has been received that **Pte. Thomas Tither** (2785) 1/5th Manchesters, 11, Daisy Hill, Westhoughton, died on August 15th at the Dardanelles from wounds received on August 3rd. Intimation had previously been received that he was wounded, and afterwards that he was in a dangerous condition. Before joining the army deceased attended the Daisy Hill Primitive Methodist Church, and in his last letter asked to be remembered to the teachers and scholars of that school. Previous to enlisting he was employed at Messrs. Fletcher, Burrows Colliery, and joined the Army shortly after the outbreak of War. He had been in the Dardanelles for several months. When he first joined the army he enlisted in the 2-5th Manchester Regiment, but changed for the 1/5th Manchesters when he went to the Dardanelles. He was a member of the Daisy Hill Football Club, though not in the playing team. In a letter to his parents, Pte. W. Gill, of the same regiment, states that whilst doing some work in the firing line Pte. Tither was caught by a sniper's bullet.

Thomas was the son of Thomas Tither b.1864, a coal miner hewer, and Hannah Tither née Cartwright b.1872.

Thomas first appeared on the 1901 Census living with his parents at 364 Wigan Road, Leigh, Lancashire.

His mother Hannah died in 1909.

By 1911 Thomas was living at 16 Mabel Street, Daisy Hill, Westhoughton with his father and siblings Elizabeth b.1904 and Joseph b.1909.

At 14 Thomas was working underground in a coal mine as a haulage hand.

His name is on Westhoughton War Memorial.

* Death recorded as 15 August on CWGC.

Name	Tither, Thomas
Rank	Private
Number	2785
Unit	5th Bn Manchester Regiment
Born	Atherton, Lancashire 22 January 1897
Enlisted	Atherton, Lancashire
Died	Alexandria, Egypt 15 August 1915
Age	18
Grave or Memorial	Chatby Military and War Cemetery, Alexandria, Egypt

Joseph Travers

Bolton Journal and Guardian 15 October 1915

Machine Gunner Killed

Private Joseph Travers, machine gun section, 1st Lancashire Fusiliers, was killed in action in Gallipoli on August 21st. He was a reservist, and was called up on the outbreak of war, being stationed for some time at Sutton-on Hull. He went to the Dardanelles on July 17th, so he had been in the trenches only a month when he met his death. He was 23 years of age, and resided with his parents at 26, Hill-st. He was a worshipper at St. Mary's Church where he was in the band, and was also a member of the Men's Club. When called up he was in the employ of Mr. Talbot, contractor, Bertand-rd., previous to which he served an apprenticeship to moulding at Musgrave's Foundry.

Joseph was the son of of Michael Travers b.1859, a carter and carrier, and Annie Travers née O'Brien b.1859.

Joseph first appeared on the 1901 Census living at 68 Smith Street, Bolton with his parents and siblings Mary Ellen b.1884, Annie b.1886, John b.1888.

By 1911 he was living at 26 Hill Street, Bolton with his parents and siblings Mary Ellen, Annie, John, Henry b.1905, James b.1907 and his uncle, John O'Brien.

Joseph was employed as an apprentice moulder at that point.

Name	Travers, Joseph
Rank	Private
Number	3641
Unit	1st Bn Lancashire Fusiliers
Born	Bolton, Lancashire c.1892
Enlisted	Bury, Lancashire
Died	Gallipoli, Turkey 21 August 1915
Age	23
Grave or Memorial	Helles Memorial, Gallipoli, Turkey

Robert Travis

Bolton Journal and Guardian 10 September 1915

Boltonians in Fierce Engagement

NORTH LANCASHIRE MEN MISSING IN GALLIPOLI

The 6th Battalion of the Loyal North Lancashire Regiment suffered in Gallipoli in an engagement on August 9th. A number of Bolton soldiers are in this Battalion…

Anxiety is also felt for the safety of **Private Robert Travis**, of 536, Blackburn-rd., Astley Bridge, of the signalling corps of the 6th Battalion, who has also been missing since August 9th. He enlisted last autumn, and was drafted to Gallipoli in June. He attended the Young Men's Class at All Soul's Sunday School, and was employed as a joiner by Mr. Pitfield, Bury New-rd. He was also well known in the Eagley area where he formerly resided.

Robert was the son of Walter Travis b.1864, a tailor, and Mary Travis née Stones b.1864.

Robert first appeared on the 1901 Census living at 196 Darwen Road, Eagley, Turton with his parents and sisters Clara b.1884, Florence Annie b.1885, Frances b.1890, Emma b.1894 and Nancy b.1898. A 4 year old boarder, Alice Wilkinson, was also a member of he household.

By 1911 he was living with his older sister Florence Annie at 121 Bridgeman Street and was working as an apprentice joiner.

The rest of the family were living at 37 Ollerton Terrace, Eagley Bank, Bolton in 1911.

Robert's name is on Dunscar War Memorial.

Name	
	Travis, Robert
Rank	
	Corporal
Number	
	11744
Unit	
	6th Bn The Loyal North Lancashire Regiment
Born	
	Eagley, Lancashire c.1892
Enlisted	
	Bolton, Lancashire
Died	
	Gallipoli, Turkey 9 August 1915
Age	
	23
Grave or Memorial	
	Helles Memorial, Gallipoli, Turkey

Ernest Tunnah

Bolton Journal and Guardian 15 October 1915

One of Three Soldier Brothers Killed

Mrs. Tunnah, 82, Soho-st., Bolton, has received an intimation that her husband, **Pte. E. Tunnah** (4154) D Company, 1st Battalion Lancashire Fusiliers, has died of wounds received on the Gallipoli Peninsula on Oct. 3rd. Pte. Tunnah, who was 26 years of age and leaves four children, was a reservist, working at Messrs. Hick, Hargreaves works, and went to the Dardanelles on July 11th. Two of his three brothers, who lived with their father at 56, James-st., are also in the Army, Albert having been sent to France in a draft from the 2/5th L.N.L. Regiment, and John being in the 4/5th L.N.L.

Ernest was the son of James Tunnah, a moulder, and Sarah Anne Tunnah.

Ernest married Annie Nolan b.1898 in Bolton in 1908.

In 1911 the couple were living at with their daughter Sarah Ann b.1909. Ernest was working as a labourer at the time.

They had three other children - James F b.1911, Lewis b.1912 and Alfred b.1914.

Name
Tunnah, Ernest
Rank
Private
Number
4154
Unit
1st Bn Lancashire Fusiliers
Born
Bolton, Lancashire 1889
Enlisted
Bury, Lancashire
Died
Gallipoli, Turkey 3 October 1915
Age
26
Grave or Memorial
East Mudros Military Cemetery, Lemnos, Greece

Albert Edward Varle

Albert was the son of John Varle b.1857, a labourer, and Catherine Varle née Fraser b.1862.

In 1891 Albert was living in Newburn, Northumberland with his parents and sisters Jessie b.1885 and Ada b.1890.

His father, John, died in 1898.

The family had moved to Bolton by 1895 but were back in Stranton, Hartlepool in 1901.

Albert also had three other siblings - Ellen b.1891, Annie b.1898 and John William b.1895.

His mother appears to have married someone called McLennen and been widowed again by 1911 when she was living in Bolton once more.

Albert enlisted in the Northumberland Fusiliers in December 1905 and transferred to the Border Regiment in August 1906. He served in New Zealand, Burma and India. By the time he left the Army in 1912 he was a Lance Corporal. He spent some time as an officer's batman. His medical examination on discharge described him as being 5' 6 1/2" tall with a fresh complexion, brown eyes and fair hair.

He returned to Bolton where, in August 1913, he got a job as a postman.

As he was still on the reserve list on the outbreak of the war he was recalled to the colours at his old rank and was rapidly promoted to Acting Sergeant.

He received a gunshot wound to his back while serving in France in December 1914 and spent some time in hospital in Aberdeen.

His mother, Catherine, was living at 3 Pike Road, Bolton in 1915.

Name	Varle, Albert Edward
Rank	Sergeant
Number	8885
Unit	1st Bn Border Regiment
Born	Stranton, Durham 1888
Enlisted	Newcastle upon Tyne December 1905
Died	Gallipoli, Turkey 21 August 1915
Age	27
Grave or Memorial	Helles Memorial, Gallipoli, Turkey

Jesse Vickers

Farnworth Weekly Journal 22 October 1915

FOOTBALLER KILLED

Mr. John Vickers, of 51, Bolton-rd., Kearsley, has received official intimation that his son, **Private Jesse Vickers** (19380) of the 6th Batt., L.N. Lancashire Regiment, was killed in action on September 9th at the Dardanelles. Pte. Vickers, who worked in the electrical department of the Chloride works at Clifton, enlisted on January 8th. He left for the front on August 28th, and must not have been in the trenches when he met his death. He had many friends in Kearsley, and was a regular attender at St. Stephen's Church, Kearsley, where the Rev. W. J. C. Scarlin, vicar on Sunday evening, made reference to his loss and the "Dead March" was played in tribute to his memory by Mr. Holden. A keen athlete, the deceased had played with several football clubs, including St. Stephen's, and last winter, before enlisting, was in the Walkden Central's team.

In his last letter home Pte. Vickers wrote: "We are doing as well as can be expected. We had a grand voyage. As I am writing we are being shelled. 'Oh, it's lovely' We get quite used to it. We are among the Indians and they are a decent lot of fellows. We are quite snug in our dug-outs. It is an old saying:'There's no place like home.' You would think so if you came out here."

Jesse was the son of John Vickers b.1864, a grocery warehouseman with the Co-operative Society, and Annie Vickers née Lindley b.1867.

In 1901 Jesse was living at 8 St Stephens Street, Kearsley with his mother and baby sister Eveline Victoria b.1901.

His other brother, Tom Vincent b.1887, was living a few doors away at 22 St Stephens Street with his other grandparents, Jesse and Elizabeth Lindley.

Jesse's father and sister Maud Emily b.1893 were visiting his grandmother Esther Vickers at 257 Manchester Road, Kearsley at the time of the Census.

Two other children - Elizabeth Annie b.1889 and Florence Hetty b.1891 died in infancy.

The 1911 Census listed Jesse as still living at 8 St Stephens Street with his parents and siblings Tom Vincent, Maud Emily and Eveline Victoria.

Jesse was employed as a cop packer in a cotton spinning mill.

His name is on Kearsley War Memorial.

George Waddilove

Bolton Journal and Guardian 17 September 1915

Former Eagley Soldier Killed in Dardanelles

Official intimation of the death of **Private George Waddilove**, 46, Primrose-st., Astley Bridge, has been received by his wife. The communication states that Private Waddilove, who was attached to the 1st Border Regiment, died from wounds on August 28th after an engagement, and this notice is supplemented by a message received by the wife of Private Robert Mason of Chorley Old-rd. (a soldier companion of Waddilove, who has also been wounded), which states that he was shot in the back on August 21st and taken to hospital. Waddilove enlisted on November 27th. He trained at Shoeburyness and was drafted to the eastern theatre of war in June. He sustained a nasty accident in the Regimental sports, severely injuring his back, which incapacitated him for several weeks. He was a native of Eagley, in which district he had always lived, prior to his marriage, and was employed as a spinner at Eagley mills, whilst he was a member of the Walmsley Unitarian Chapel and School. The deceased soldier leaves a wife and two children aged five and three. He was 31 years of age.

George was the son of Thomas Waddilove b.1858, a cotton spinner, and Emily Annie Waddilove née Bates b.1862.

George first appeared on the 1891 Census living at 11 Longworth Mill Cottages, Astley Bridge, Bolton with his parents and siblings Harriet b.1886 and Oscar b.1889.

George's mother Emily died later in 1891 and his father remarried to Sarah Sumner in 1893.

In 1901 George was living at 21 Hough Lane, Eagley with his father and stepmother, his siblings Harriet, Oscar, Ann b.1892, Beatrice b.1895 and Amelia b.1899 and the children of his stepmother, George, Jane and Alice Sumner.

George married Florence Isherwood b.1887 at Christ Church, Walmsley on 15 August 1908.

In 1911 the couple were living at 44 Primrose Street, Astley Bridge, Bolton.

George was working as an operative cotton spinner.

They had two children, including George b.1913.

He died on board HS Alaunia from wounds received in action (gunshot wound to abdomen) and was buried at sea. His personal effects as returned to his wife were:

1 pocket wallet

correspondence

7 photos

10 picture postcards

1 purse

1 cigarette case

1 pocket knife

2 pencils

George's name is on Dunscar War Memorial.

Name	Waddilove, George
Rank	Private
Number	18181
Unit	1st Bn Border Regiment
Born	Bolton, Lancashire c.1884
Enlisted	Bolton, Lancashire 27 November 1914
Died	Gallipoli, Turkey 28 August 1915
Age	31
Grave or Memorial	Buried at sea - Helles Memorial, Gallipoli, Turkey

Name
Walker, James
Rank
Private
Number
7552
Unit
1st Bn
Border Regiment
Born
Bolton, Lancashire
c.1885
Enlisted
Manchester
Died
Gallipoli, Turkey
30 April 1915
Age
31
Grave or Memorial
Helles Memorial,
Gallipoli, Turkey

James Walker

Bolton Journal and Guardian 14 May 1915

Killed in the Dardanelles

News has been received that a Bolton soldier has lost his life in the severe fighting in the Dardanelles. He is **Private James Walker**, 1st Battalion, Border Regiment, who formerly lived with his parents at 3 Webster-st. He was 31 years of age and had served in the army for 11 years, having been in India for 8 years. Private Walker was formerly employed at Messrs. Charles Heaton and Son's mill, Weston-st.

James appeared on the 1911 Census as a private soldier stationed in Burma with the 1st Bn Border Regiment.

William Walker

Bolton Journal and Guardian 10 September 1915

Boltonians in Fierce Engagement

NORTH LANCASHIRE MEN MISSING IN GALLIPOLI

The 6th Battalion of the Loyal North Lancashire Regiment suffered in Gallipoli in an engagement on August 9th. A number of Bolton soldiers are in this Battalion…

After the same engagement **Corporal William Walker**, also of the 6th Battalion, and formerly of 34, Horrocks-st, Valletts, is also reported missing. He went through the same training as Mather and Travis, and has been through several previous engagements. Before enlisting he worked at Mortfield Bleachworks. He was a regular attender at St. Peter's Mission, Valletts He is only 19 years of age, and gained his first stripe during his first three months of training. He has three other brothers serving with the colours in France, one having been on active service since the beginning of the war.

William was the son of William Walker b.1860, a scavenger for Bolton Corporation and Eliza Ann Walker née Roscoe b.1864.

William first appeared on the 1901 Census living at 95 Valletts Lane with his parents and siblings Jane b.1886, Peter b.1889, Maggie b.1891, Alice b.1895, and Richard b.1899.

By 1911 he was living at 34 Horrocks Street, Bolton with his parents and brothers Peter and Richard.

Name	Walker, William
Rank	Corporal
Number	11161
Unit	6th Bn The Loyal North Lancashire Regiment
Born	Bolton, Lancashire c.1896
Enlisted	Bolton, Lancashire
Died	Gallipoli, Turkey 9 August 1915
Age	19
Grave or Memorial	Basra Memorial, Iraq

George Warren

Bolton Journal and Guardian 31 December 1915

Edgworth Soldier Killed

The villages of Turton and Edgworth have learned with regret this Christmas of the death in action of **Private George Warren**, son of Mr. Warren, who for many years has been gardener at the Edgworth Children's Home. The sad notification has been received from the War Office, together with the expression of regret for the King and Queen. Private Warren was exceedingly well known in the village, and his sunny and genial disposition endeared him to all who knew him. He enlisted on October 26th, 1914, when 17 years of age, and on his 18th birthday was en route for the Dardanelles. He joined the army as a member of the R.A.M.C. After a few months' training at Aldershot he was moved to Wales, and ultimately transferred to the 2nd Battalion South Wales Borderers. In this Battalion he completed his training at Liverpool, and on August 15th sailed for the Dardanelles. Beyond the official intimation that he was killed in action no other hews is to hand. In civilian life he was employed at Know Mill Printing Company. These works have already one killed and one missing on the roll of honour. Private Warren was a very clever swimmer and diver, and in 1913 he was the winner of two silver cups and five medals. At Bolton he won the first medal for diving, and the first for life-saving at Haslingden. He was also instrumental in saving a life. At Morecambe he was first in the diving competition, diving 20 feet, whilst a similar award was granted him at Liverpool for diving, and also for swimming. He carried off the silver cup, and a championship medal for diving at Granton (Scotland), and won the second silver cup for a quarter mile race at London. Many expressions of sympathy have been received by the family, and these have done much to ease the terrible shock to them. Private Warren was a regular attender at the Brotherhood, and a worshipper at the Wesleyan Chapel, where a memorial service will be held on Sunday next. At the Parish Church, on Sunday last the "Dead March" was played in honour of the deceased soldier. Three Turton and Edgworth soldiers and sailors have now lost their lives, and one is missing.

George was the son of John Warren b.1855, gardener at Edgworth Children's Home, and Mary Warren b.1853.

In 1901 George was living at Garden Cottage, Edgworth Children's Home with his parents and siblings Pollie b.1879, John b.1881, Nellie b.1882, Henry b.1886, Minnie b.1889, Florrie b.1892 and William b.1895.

George was still living at the Children's Home in 1911 with his parents and siblings Henry, Florrie, and William.

Name
Warren, George
Rank
Private
Number
3/24825
Unit
2nd Bn South Wales Borderers
Born
Edgworth, Lancashire 1897
Enlisted
Bolton, Lancashire 26 October 1914
Died
Gallipoli, Turkey 2 December 1915
Age
18
Grave or Memorial
Skew Bridge Cemetery, Helles, Gallipoli, Turkey

Thomas Westby

Bolton Journal and Guardian 1 October 1915

Comrades Notify Westhoughton Man's Death

Mrs. Westby, 4, Manchester-rd., Westhoughton, has received official intimation from the Record Office, Cork, of the death of her husband, **Private T. Westby** (3833), of the 5th Batt., Connaught Rangers. He enlisted in the Connaughts in Bolton last February, and after training in Ireland, his battalion was sent with the Mediterranean Expeditionary Force. He has written frequent letters home telling of his experiences in the Gallipoli fighting, and the last time his wife heard from him was in a letter written on August 5th, stating he was well and happy. He was reported, by his comrades, to have been killed on August 21st, although his name had not been notified from official sources. Mrs. Westby asked for information from his regimental record office, however, and the sad news is now confirmed. Deceased, who was only 26 years of age, was employed by the Wigan Coal and Canal Co., Westhoughton. He leaves a wife and young child.

Thomas married Jane Caldwell b.1880 in Bolton in 1910.

In 1911 the couple were living at 16 Smithy Street, Westhoughton with their son John b.1911.

Thomas was working as a coal miner.

Name
Westby, Thomas
Rank
Private
Number
3833
Unit
5th Bn Connaught Rangers
Born
Bolton, Lancashire 1889
Enlisted
Bolton, Lancashire
Died
Gallipoli, Turkey 21 August 1915
Age
26
Grave or Memorial
Helles Memorial, Gallipoli, Turkey

James Whitworth

Bolton Journal and Guardian 27 August 1915

Killed by Sniper in Gallipoli

News has been received by his parents that **Pte. James Whitworth**, Border Regiment, whose home is at 3, Osborne-grove, Bolton, has been killed in Gallipoli. The information comes from a friend of the deceased's, Private Herbert Leyland who says he was killed by a Turkish sniper at 5.00 a. m. on August 2nd. Deceased would have been 22 years of age on August 3rd. He enlisted in the first week of this year, and went to the Dardanelles during the Bolton holiday week. He was employed by the Haslam Spinning Company, and attended Park-st Wesleyan Chapel and schools. His brother Alfred is also in the Border Regiment, but is still in England.

James was the son of Alfred Whitworth b.1867, an iron moulder, and Emma Whitworth née Houlder b.1856.

James first appeared on the 1901 Census living at 16 Regent Street, Bolton with his parents and siblings Elizabeth Alice b.1887, Alfred b.1889, Susannah b.1891, Polly b.1892, Arthur b.1895, William b.1897, Emma b.1899 and Ellen b.1900.

By 1911 he was living at with his parents and siblings as above with the addition of sister Annie b.1903.

James was working as a bander in a cotton mill.

His friend and fellow Boltonian, Herbert Leyland, survived Gallipoli but was killed in action in France on 1 July 1916.

Name	
Whitworth, James	
Rank	
Private	
Number	
19076	
Unit	
"B" Coy 1st Bn Border Regiment	
Born	
Bolton, Lancashire 1893	
Enlisted	
Bolton, Lancashire January 1915	
Died	
Gallipoli, Turkey 2 August 1915	
Age	
22	
Grave or Memorial	
Twelve Tree Copse Cemetery, Gallipoli, Turkey	

John Wildman

Farnworth Weekly Journal 24 September 1915

Farnworth Soldier Killed

Mrs. Wildman, of Lea Farm, Highfield, Farnworth, received official intimation on Tuesday morning of the death of her son, **Private John William* Wildman** (19077), aged 22 years, of the 1st battalion Border Regiment. It was stated that he was killed in action at the Dardanelles on August 21st, on the same date as several other local soldiers. He was a moulder at Messrs. Bennis's Ironworks at Little Hulton. He enlisted on January 7th, and after training in Essex, went to the East in July. Private F. Greenhalgh, of 176 Clegg-lane, in a letter home written on August 28th says he had seen nothing of Wildman since they made the big advance.

At the same time that Pte. Wildman was killed, his pal and cousin, Pte. Harry Hooper, of 427 Plodder-lane, who enlisted with him, was wounded in the arm. He has been taken to hospital, and is progressing favourably. Both men were associated with St. George's Day and Sunday Schools.

John was the eldest son of John Thomas Wildman b.1867, a farmer, and Mary Wildman née Eckersley b.1874.

John first appeared on the 1901 Census living at Lea Farm, Highfield, Farnworth with his parents and brothers Harry b.1895, Clifford b.1897 and George b.1900. The family also employed a cattleman who lived with them.

John's father died in 1908.

In 1911 John was living at the farm with his mother and siblings Harry, Clifford, George, Alice b.1903 and Arthur b.1905. The family also employed a live-in waggoner.

While Harry and Clifford were working on the farm, John was employed as a moulder's apprentice.

John's name is on Farnworth War Memorial.

* He is not referred to as John William on any other record.

Name	Wildman, John
Rank	Private
Number	19077
Unit	1st Bn Border Regiment
Born	Farnworth, Lancashire 1893
Enlisted	Bolton, Lancashire 7 January 1915
Died	Gallipoli, Turkey 21 August 1915
Age	22
Grave or Memorial	Green Hill Cemetery, Gallipoli, Turkey

Thomas Wilkinson

Bolton Journal and Guardian 5 November 1915

Killed in Mediterranean

Mr. Charles Wilkinson, 22, Villiers-st., Bolton, has received news that his brother, **Pt. Thos. Wilkinson**, 9th Battalion, Lancashire Fus., was killed in the Mediterranean on October 9th. Prior to the war Wilkinson had served five years with the Navy and enlisted in the Lancashire Fus. Last August. He resided at 17, Heywood's Hollow, Astley Bridge, and worked at Messrs. Dobson and Barlow's.

Thomas was the son of John Thomas Wilkinson b.1860, a self-actor minder in a cotton mill, and Rachel Wilkinson née Paulden b.1862

Thomas first appeared on the 1891 Census living at 15 Coop Street, Astley Bridge, Bolton with his parents and brother Charles b.1887. Thomas's grandmother, Mary Wilkinson was also visiting the family.

Thomas's mother Rachel died in the summer of 1891.

Thomas's father remarried to Ellen Birch b.1877 in 1896.

In 1901 Thomas and Charles were living at 56 Old Road, Astley Bridge, Bolton with their paternal grandmother Mary Wilkinson, a retail grocer. The brothers were both employed as cotton piecers at the time.

Thomas's father was living next door at 54 Old Road with wife Ellen and children Harry b.1899 and John b.1901.

In 1911 Charles was still serving in the Royal Navy as a First Class Stoker and was visiting his brother Charles and his wife Jessie at the family home of Jessie's parents (Richard and Mary Ann Jones), 15-16 Heywood's Hollow, Astley Bridge, Bolton.

Name	
Wilkinson, Thomas	
Rank	
Private	
Number	
3161	
Unit	
9th Bn Lancashire Fusiliers	
Born	
Bolton, Lancashire c.1889	
Enlisted	
Bury, Lancashire	
Died	
Gallipoli, Turkey 9 October 1915	
Age	
26	
Grave or Memorial	
Helles Memorial, Gallipoli, Turkey	

Albert Edward Williams

Bolton Journal and Guardian 23 July 1915

Died Two Days before His Birthday

Information was received to-day by his wife who with their two children reside at 16, Radcliffe-rd., Haulgh, that her husband, **Pte. Albert Edwin** (sic) **Williams**, has died of wounds received in the fighting in the Dardanelles. Pte. Williams, who died on 29th June, two days before his 28th birthday, enlisted at the Town Hall the week before Christmas in the Royal Dublin Fusiliers. He had been in the Dardanelles area for about 10 weeks. In civil life the gallant soldier was employed at Messrs. Walmsley's Forge.

Albert was the son of Richard Williams b.1854, a puddler in a an iron forge, and Margaret Elizabeth Williams née Beddow b.1859.

Albert first appeared on the 1891 Census living at 6 Burlington Street, Bolton with his parents and siblings Alice b.1878, Mary Jane b.1882, William b.1894, Thomas b.1896, and Sarah b.1890.

In 1901 Albert was living at 15 Jenny Beck Street, Bolton with his parents and siblings Richard b.1884 (who wasn't present on the previous Census) Alice, Mary Jane, Thomas, Sarah, Elizabeth b.1893, Ruth b.1895, Agnes b.1897 and Harry b.1900.

Albert was working as a piecer in a cotton mill at that point.

Albert married Annie Harris b.1889 at St Peter's Church, Bolton on 1 May 1909.

Name
Williams, Albert Edward
Rank
Private
Number
17750
Unit
1st Bn Royal Dublin Fusiliers
Born
Bolton, Lancashire 1 July 1887
Enlisted
Bolton, Lancashire
Died
Gallipoli, Turkey 29 June 1915
Age
27
Grave or Memorial
Twelve Tree Copse Cemetery, Gallipoli, Turkey

William Wilson

Bolton Journal and Guardian 14 May 1915

Local Marine Dies of Wounds

Official intimation has been received by Mrs Mayoh, 11, Minerva-st., with whom he resided, that her nephew, **Pte. William Wilson** has died of wounds sustained on May 5th whilst serving with the Royal Marine Light Infantry near the Dardanelles. Wilson, who was 33 years of age, enlisted in October, and previous to being sent out was in training at Plymouth. He formerly worked as a roller-turner at Messrs. Ryder's, Folds-rd., and was a regular attender at St John's Church and Sunday School. A pathetic feature of the occurrence is that a letter was received from the deceased this morning asking his aunt to "put a wreath on pa's grave."

William died of wounds at 'Y' Beach. His body was brought on board the Hospital Ship Guildford Castle.

His next of kin was listed as a friend, Mrs Mayoh, 11 Minerva Street, Bolton.

Name
Wilson, William
Rank
Private
Number
PLY/459(S)
Unit
Plymouth Bn Royal Naval Division, Royal Marine Light Infantry
Born
Preston, Lancashire 19 December 1892
Enlisted
Died
Gallipoli, Turkey 26 April 1915
Age
22
Grave or Memorial
Plymouth Naval Memorial, Plymouth, Devon

Samuel Wolstencroft

Bolton Journal and Guardian 5 November 1915

Shot Through the Head

Mr. Wolsoncroft, of Oak-st., Farnworth, received official intimation on Sunday that his son, **Private S. Wolsoncroft***(27026), of the 8th Battalion Welsh Regiment, was killed on August 14th at the Dardanelles. The news was not unexpected, for a comrade in arms, Pte. H. Topping, of Royley Row, Kearsley, had sent word that Wolsoncroft had been shot through the head by a Turkish sniper a few days after they had made a bayonet charge, The deceased, who was 21* years of age, enlisted at Walkden on September 14th last year in the 6th L.N.L. Regiment, and was transferred to the Welsh Regiment after six months' training. He went out to the East about four months ago. Like his father he worked at Messrs. Harrison Blair's Kearsley Chemical Works, where he was serving his apprenticeship as a plumber. He was a footballer, having played with a Moses Gate club, and was on the roll of honour at both St. Peter's and All Saints' Churches.

Samuel was the son of Thomas Wolstencroft b.1872, a labourer at a chemical works, and Emily Wolstencroft née Fletcher.

Samuel first appeared on the 1901 Census living at 39 Cooke Street, Farnworth with his parents and sister Alice b.1898.

In 1911 he was living at 37 Lark Hill, Farnworth with his parents and siblings Alice, Martha b.1901 and Thomas b.1906.

Samuel was working as a chemical plumber's apprentice.

His name is on Farnworth War Memorial.

* CWGC incorrectly records him as Samuel Wolsoncroft, as in the newspaper article.

Name	
Wolstencroft, Samuel	
Rank	
Private	
Number	
27026	
Unit	
8th Bn Welsh Regiment	
Born	
Bolton, Lancashire c.1896	
Enlisted	
Farnworth, Lancashire	
Died	
Gallipoli, Turkey 16 August 1915	
Age	
19	
Grave or Memorial	
Helles Memorial, Gallipoli, Turkey	

Robert Wood

Bolton Journal and Guardian

Darcy Lever Soldier's Death

The parents of **Robert Wood**, 99, Radcliffe-rd., Bank-terrace, Darcy Lever, have just received sad notification of his death from wounds. He was only 22 years of age and enlisted last December, at the Bolton Town hall, in the Royal Dublin Fusiliers. He crossed the day after his attestation to Ireland, where he went through his training, and when his regiment was moved to the Dardanelles, on May 7th he had never had a furlough and his friends at home never had the opportunity of seeing him in khaki. He was formerly a piecer at the Lever Bridge Mill of Messrs. Wm. Gray and Son. Ltd., and was a scholar at St. Stephen and All Martyrs' School, and was well-known in the district.

Robert was the son of Edward Wood b.1870, a colliery fireman, and Nancy Ellen Wood née Faulkner b.1870.

Robert first appeared on the 1901 Census living at 70 Hacken Lane with his parents and siblings Mary Ann b.1892, Robert b.1894, William b.1896 and Sydney b.1899.

The family were living at the same address in 1911 with the addition of children Joseph b.1902 and Emily b.1904.

Robert was employed as a side piecer in a textile mill.

Name
Wood, Robert
Rank
Private
Number
17479
Unit
1st Bn Royal Dublin Fusiliers
Born
Bolton, Lancashire c.1893
Enlisted
Bolton, Lancashire December 1914
Died
Gallipoli, Turkey 28 September 1915
Age
22
Grave or Memorial
Hill 10 Cemetery, Gallipoli, Turkey

William Henry Woodall

Bolton Journal and Guardian 24 November 1916

Missing since August 9th, 1915, **Pte. WILLIAM HENRY WOODALL**, Loyal North Lancashire Regiment, has been officially presumed to have died on that date in the Gallipoli campaign. He joined soon after the declaration of war, being previously engaged as a marker-up at Messrs. Barlow's, Manchester. Woodall, who leaves a widow and two children at 111, Kay-st., Bolton, was 30* years of age. He is supposed to have perished in the landing at Suvla Bay.

William was the son of William Henry Woodall b.1860, a maker up of cotton goods, and Elizabeth Ann Woodall, née Waddicar b.1859.

He first appeared on the 1891 Census living at 117 Mill Hill Street with his parents and brother Charles b.1890. His paternal uncle Charles Woodall b.1855 was living with the family.

In 1901 the family (without Uncle Charles) were living at 45 Cemetery Road, Breightmet, Bolton. William jnr was employed as a piecer in a cotton mill.

His mother Elizabeth died in 1907.

William married Mary Elizabeth (Lizzie) Hardman b.1888 at All Souls Church, Bolton on 27 June 1908.

* *William was 28 years old when he died.*

Name	
Woodall, William Henry	
Rank	
Private	
Number	
10975	
Unit	
6th Bn The Loyal North Lancashire Regiment	
Born	
Bolton, Lancashire 1887	
Enlisted	
Bolton, Lancashire	
Died	
Gallipoli, Turkey 9 August 1915	
Age	
28	
Grave or Memorial	
Helles Memorial, Gallipoli, Turkey	

Alan Woodley

Bolton Journal and Guardian 6 August 1915

Another Hero of the Dardanelles

Mr. P. Woodley, secretary of the Queen's Picture Theatre Company, who resides in Sutherland-rd, New Hall-lane, Bolton, has received word from the Admiralty that his son, **Alan**, died from wounds on July 19th in the Dardanelles. The deceased soldier who was in the Royal Marine Light Infantry (Plymouth Battalion) was 21 years of age, and enlisted in October last. Prior to that he was employed as chief operator at the Queen's Picture House.

Alan was the son of George Thomas Burr Woodley b.1866 and Emma Woodley née Williamson b.1866.

Alan first appeared on the 1901 Census living at 25 Beckett Road, Wheatley, Yorkshire with his parents and sister Margaret b.1900. George was working as a colliery clerk at the time.

By 1911 Alan was living at 200 West Terrace, Burley in Wharfedale, Yorkshire as a boarder with the family of Harry and Annie Smith while working as a chemist's assistant.

In 1911 his parents were living in Hunslet, Yorkshire where George was running a grocery business at three different addresses. Margaret was living with her Aunt and Uncle's family in Oldham.

Alan died on board the Hospital Ship 'Rewa' from wounds received in action.

John William Worsley

Bolton Journal and Guardian 17 September 1915

More 6th Lancashire Losses after Suvla Bay Landing

Still another Bolton man is notified as missing from the the 6th L.N.L. Regiment after the terrible engagement on August 9th in Gallipoli. He is **Private** (12117) **J. W. Worsley**, a single man, whose mother lives at 256, Lever-st., and who left his job in Canada to enlist in the home country at the beginning of the war. He served seven years in the Militia, but before going to Canada, two and a half years ago, he was employed by Messrs. Joshua Crook and Sons, ltd,. Deane-rd,. as a side piecer, and his name appears on the roll of honour in Connexion with St. Mark's Church. Another brother, Joseph Worsley, of the 2nd Batt. Lancashire Fusiliers,was in the fighting at Mons, and is a prisoner in the Doberitz Camp.

John was the son of Robert Worsley b.1845, a cotton piecer, and Emma Worsley née Ridings b.1851.

John first appeared on the 1881 Census as a baby living at 23 Chapel Street, Bolton with his parents and sisters Margaret Alice b.1874, Sarah b.1875 and Jane b.1878.

In 1891 John was living at 6 Back Slaterfield in the household of Joseph Wild with his mother and siblings James b.1884 Elizabeth Emma b.1887 and Joseph b.1890.

John's father Robert was living at 8 Barlow Street, Bolton with John's older sisters Margaret Alice, Sarah and Jane.

In 1901 John was living at 17 Coe Street, Bolton - once again in the household of Joseph Wild and with his mother (styling herself as a widow) and siblings Elizabeth Emma and Joseph.

Robert was then living at 67 Well Street with his daughter Jane who by this time was married to Thomas E Jackson.

By 1911 John was living at 33 Back Slaterfield. Bolton with his mother.

He was working as cotton spinner.

Robert was still living with daughter Jane in the Jackson household.

Name	
Worsley, John William	
Rank	
Private	
Number	
12117	
Unit	
6th Bn The Loyal North Lancashire Regiment	
Born	
Great Lever, Lancashire 1881	
Enlisted	
Bolton, Lancashire 27 August 1914	
Died	
Gallipoli, Turkey 9 August 1915	
Age	
34	
Grave or Memorial	
Helles Memorial, Gallipoli, Turkey	

John Worsley

Bolton Journal and Guardian 24 September 1915

Killed by Shrapnel

Mr. and Mrs. Worsley, 114, Blackburn-rd., have been notified that their son, **Private J. Worsley** (5073), 1st Lancashire Fusiliers, was killed in action on August 22nd. Private Worsley was 32 years of age, and in civil life was employed at the Globe Ironworks of Messrs. J. Musgrave and Sons, Ltd. He had completed seven years in the Militia at Ashton-under-Lyne, and at the beginning of the war war again offered his services but was rejected. So keen, however, was his desire to volunteer that he went to Bury, and was accepted for the Fusiliers. After training at Barrow-in-Furness he was drafted to the Dardanelles on July 3rd, and while in Gallipoli he met many Bolton boys. In describing how Private Worsley met his death by a burst of shrapnel on Sunday, August 22nd, Sergt-Major Carr writes saying that the battalion had been hard worked during the battle, which was prolonged to mid-day on the 22nd. On the night of the 22nd the battalion was moving to a resting place when they were shelled by the Turks, Private Worsley being killed. "We buried him," says Sergt-Major Carr, "as respectfully as we could under darkness, and, as comrades always do, with the greatest of sympathy."

John was the son of John Worsley b.1852, a furniture broker, and Mary Anne Worsley née Morley b.1849.

Name	
Worsley, John	
Rank	Private
Number	5073
Unit	1st Bn Lancashire Fusiliers
Born	Bolton, Lancashire c.1883
Enlisted	Bury, Lancashire
Died	Gallipoli, Turkey 22 August 1915
Age	32
Grave or Memorial	Helles Memorial, Gallipoli, Turkey

Herbert Yates

Bolton Journal and Guardian 10 September 1915

Boltonians in Fierce Engagement

NORTH LANCASHIRE MEN MISSING IN GALLIPOLI

The 6th Battalion of the Loyal North Lancashire Regiment suffered in Gallipoli in an engagement on August 9th. A number of Bolton soldiers are in this Battalion…

Private Herbert Yates (11190), 6th L. N. L. has been posted as missing after an engagement in Gallipoli, on August 9th, 1915. He lived with his wife in Bolton at 20, Haigh-st., and was employed at Messrs, Dobson and Barlow's. He enlisted at the latter part of August last year and underwent training at Preston, Tidworth, and Blackdown. He has two other brothers in the Army, one of whom is home wounded. The other has just completed his last leave and is stationed at Aldershot.

Bolton Journal and Guardian 14 July 1916

Missing, Now Presumed Dead

Private Herbert Yates (11190), Loyal North Lancashires, has been missing since August 9th, 1915 and now the War Office has intimated to his wife, who resides at 49, Union-rd., Tonge Moor, that it is assumed that he died on that date. Yates enlisted on August 14th, 1914, and went into training at Tidworth, Winchester, and Blackdown. From the latter place he went to the Dardanelles on June 14th, 1915. Yates, who was 32 years of age, worked in the ring spindle department at Messrs. Dobson and Barlow's until he joined the Army. He attended Mawdsley-st. P.S.A.* and his name appears on the Roll of Honour. He leaves a widow and one child.

Herbert was the son of William Yates b.1841, a general labourer, and Alice Yates née Rose b.1845.

Herbert first appeared on the 1891 Census living at 17 Frazer Street, Bolton with his parents and siblings Ann Rose b.1871, Edward b.1875, Henry b.1878, Mary b.1880, Goodman b.1882, Louisa b.1886, Samuel b.1888 and Albert b.1890.

In 1901 Herbert was living at 8 Herbert Street, Bolton with his widowed mother and siblings Louisa, Samuel and Albert along with married sister Ann Hamer and her three children.

Herbert married Mary Ellen Carson b.1885 at All Souls Church, Bolton on 2 April 1904.

In 1911 the couple were living at 4 Boston Street, Bolton with their daughter Mary Ellen b.1905 and Herbert's brother Albert.

* PSA = Pleasant Sunday Afternoon

Name
Yates, Herbert
Rank
Private
Number
11190
Unit
6th Bn The Loyal North Lancashire Regiment
Born
Bolton, Lancashire c.1884
Enlisted
Bolton, Lancashire August 1914
Died
Gallipoli, Turkey 9 August 1915
Age
31
Grave or Memorial
Helles Memorial, Gallipoli, Turkey

Name	
Yates, Tom Fletcher	
Rank	
Private	
Number	
1904	
Unit	
1st/5th Bn	
Lancashire Fusiliers	
Born	
Kearsley, Lancashire	
1895	
Enlisted	
Bury, Lancashire	
Died	
Gallipoli, Turkey	
7 August 1915	
Age	
20	
Grave or Memorial	
Helles Memorial	
Gallipoli, Turkey	

Tom Fletcher Yates

Tom was the son of John Yates b.1861, a cotton warp dresser, and Mary Yates née Fletcher b.1864.

In 1901 Tom was living at 133 High Street, Little Lever with his parents and siblings Harry b.1886, David b.1892, Ethel b.1893 and Lewis b.1900.

By 1911 Tom was living at 102 Stand Lane, Radcliffe, Lancashire with his parents and siblings David, Ethel and Lewis. Harry appears to have died by this point along with two other children.

Tom was working as an apprentice iron fitter.